Diana Batterlee

As our culture increasingly glorifies outward appearances and the perfect body image, we need a book that helps us stay grounded and look past the comparisons and lies. Most women long to feel confident about the way they look. In her book *Comfortable in Your Own Skin*, Debi Newman helps women of all ages gain a fresh and honest understanding of their true beauty in Christ. Her words of wisdom and encouragement speak to the core issues of a woman's heart and help every woman gain a healthy new perspective of lasting beauty.

—KAROL LADD, Author of *The Power of a Positive Woman*

Every woman should read this book and absorb the truth and wisdom of how God created our bodies and souls to project an inner beauty that comes only from His glory. With biblical teaching, anecdotal evidence, and practical counsel, Newman's book has greatly helped me heal from a destructive body image to one that is realistic and lifegiving. Staying healthy is a lifelong process, and thanks to *Comfortable in Your Own Skin* I'm on the path!

—LUCINDA SECREST MCDOWELL, Speaker and Author
of *Spa for the Soul*

Women today face a never-ending media barrage promoting a completely unrealistic image of the female body. As a result, far too many Christians have fallen prey to a never-ending cycle of dieting and despair that leads almost inevitably to self-loathing. Others have given up and completely neglect their bodies. What women desperately need is a balanced approach to caring for our bodies, which are, after all, the only living sacrifice we have to offer God. In *Comfortable in Your Own Skin*, Dr. Deborah Newman takes a compassionate approach, challenging readers to release unrealistic expectations while embracing both a healthy mind-set and a healthy lifestyle.

—DONNA PARTOW, Author of *Becoming the Woman I Want to Be*

comfortable
in your own skin

making peace with
your body image

Tyndale House Publishers, Inc., Carol Stream, Illinois DR. DEBORAH NEWMAN

A Focus on the Family book published by
Tyndale House Publishers, Inc., Carol Stream, Illinois 60188

TYNDALE and Tyndale's quill logo are registered trademarks of Tyndale House
Publishers, Inc.

The case examples presented in this book are fictional composites based on the author's
clinical experience with hundreds of clients through the years. Any resemblance between
these fictional characters and actual persons is coincidental.

Library of Congress Cataloging-in-Publication Data

ISBN-10: 1-58997-354-2
ISBN-13: 978-1-58997-354-1

Edited by: Kathy Davis
Cover design by: Jennifer Ghionzoli
Cover photographs © by Photos.com. All rights reserved.

Printed in the United States of America
1 2 3 4 5 6 7 8 9 / 13 12 11 10 09 08 07

Contents

Acknowledgments

This is a book I needed to write because I have a passion in my heart for the many women and girls who are being seduced by lies. My heart is concerned for future generations because they will be at greater risk of body despair. I pray this book will be a life-changing tool that will equip readers with the truth of God's Word and will serve to inspire women to resist the culture's clutch on their self-esteem.

The Focus on the Family creative team partnered with me in accomplishing this task. I'm grateful to the many people who worked behind the scenes at Focus on the Family on the 2002 project, including Mark Maddox, Kathy Davis, Julie Küss, Liz Duckworth, and Mary Houser. In this updated work, credit is due to Nanci McAlister, Kathy Davis, and the current staff.

Most of all, I want to acknowledge so many of you who gave testimony to the ways God transformed your lives after reading the first book. Your feedback is the main reason we have created this six-week, life-changing Bible study.

My husband, Brian, was my silent partner supplying research assistance, encouragement, grocery shopping, carpooling, and anything else that was needed. You're the greatest! I'm also so blessed to have two wonderful and understanding children, Rachel and Ben. Thanks for doing your part.

I'm grateful that God has allowed me this wonderful privilege to minister to women. "For it is God who is at work in you, both to will and to work for His good pleasure" (Philippians 2:13, NASB).

An Invitation to Freedom

arybeth was asked to model in the fashion show the women's ministry in her church was sponsoring to raise money for its spring retreat. Her answer was typical for Marybeth: "I couldn't do that." She said it sweetly and seemed so humble. No one would have suspected that at age 49, as a grandmother-to-be with two grown daughters, Marybeth was a very insecure women. Although she was one of the best-dressed women at church, deep inside she harbored a tremendous vault filled with body hate that bordered on disgust.

Beneath her quick reply, "I couldn't do that," lay this painful thought: *How could you even suggest such a thing! The last thing I would do is walk onto a stage inviting people to look at me. I don't need anyone else to look at every bulge or inspect my latest wrinkle. Believe me, I can do that all by myself.*

Marybeth's dilemma is made all the more significant by the fact that Christine, who took her place, was a 38-year-old, overweight mother of three who was honored to be asked. She thought nothing of walking her size-18 body down the runway of the church. She enjoyed every minute of it. Christine knows that she needs to lose some weight and recently started a workout program. But just because she doesn't have the perfect body doesn't mean she's not comfortable in it—especially in the company of her friends.

I've struggled all my life to accept
myself because of my weight.

Marybeth's and Christine's differences in body perspectives came to mind one day as I sat in my counseling office across from Susan. She was an attractive 16-year-old. Although she was not being pursued by top modeling agencies, she was above average in appearance. Her thick, naturally blonde hair had a slight wave. She was five feet four inches and wore a size 9. Susan was on the drill team at school and took dance lessons twice a week so she could keep ahead of the competition for her coveted spot.

So why was Susan in my counseling office? Because she was depressed, which she admitted to her mom, but she was also in the first stages of bulimia, which she could barely admit to herself.

As Susan told me about her life and her problem with depression, I got a little angry inside. I was not angry at Susan; I was angry about the outrageous pressure to look perfect that Susan faced every day. I was mad because a wonderful creation of God stared at herself in Lycra 10 to 12 hours a week and cringed at her appearance.

It struck me a little more poignantly as I listened to Susan describe her body. She told me that her only positive physical characteristic was her big brown eyes. What she hated most about herself was her height and her midsection. She wanted to be six feet tall and lose a few pounds and thin out through her stomach, hips, and thighs. I've heard all that before, but the way she talked about her arms got to me. She hated the way her flabby arms waved in the wind!

For two decades as a Christian counselor, I've listened to girls and women describe their body hate. They've focused mainly on their hips, stomach, thighs, and breasts. But in the same week I met with Susan, I also heard two other females, one 40 years old and another teenager, complain about their arms!

When is it going to stop? I despise hearing this same painful story repeated over and over. It begins as predictably as, "Once upon a time," except there is no "happily ever after." There's something about each woman's body that doesn't quite fit with her perception of what's beautiful. Whether she is too short, her thighs are too big, or her breasts are too small or too saggy, a woman's body hate can lead to depression, eating disorders, and unnecessary surgery. This kind of preoccupation with her appearance can even be fatal through suicide, botched surgery, or deadly complications from eating disorders. It is a serious problem.

It's difficult to have problems with vision
and hearing as I get older.

The teenage years have always been a period of preoccupation with looks. This fixation is even more serious in the twenty-first century. But it is no longer confined to the teen and young adult years. Some women, like Marybeth, struggle with an unhealthy obsession about their looks all their lives. We can't ignore this problem that is wreaking havoc in the lives of girls, teenagers, and women.

I've got to help fight the body-hating insanity I find all around me. I can help one person at a time in my counseling office, but I feel compelled to do more—to sound a warning, to challenge women and girls to get together and talk about the problem, to confront the lies, and to support one another in living in the truth. My hope is to help mothers consider this issue in their lives so they are able to help their daughters live in dignity, not self-imposed disgrace. I long for women in the church to reveal to a confused and mixed-up world how God's love, purpose, and acceptance transcend cultural pressure to look good!

That's why I've written this book. That's why I'm glad you are joining with me in fighting for truth, first within yourself, and then by teaching others. Together we can take a stand against negative body stress! In my years of experience I have witnessed how God's Word, taught in the context of supportive relationships, dramatically transforms lives. If the Marybeths, Christines, and Susans will sit down together and discover the truth about their bodies through studying God's Word, they can stop the epidemic of body hate and keep it from devastating their own and others' lives.

Breast cancer has changed almost every part of my body for the worse: My skin is dry, my hair is thinner, my breasts aren't real. But it has also helped me focus on what is really important, and it isn't all that other stuff.

I am thrilled that you are reading this book. I can't wait for you to learn the joy of liking and being at peace with the body you live in. I doubt that you are even aware of how much a negative body image can affect you. God has so much He wants to show you about the meaning of your life and His perspective on your body. In the culture we live in, I believe it is critical for women to think about and discuss this subject.

This is a good book for you to read on your own, but I have purposely written it to be experienced with a group. In my years as a counselor, I have witnessed the healing power of group interaction. Women, in particular, heal through relationship and connection to other women—God designed us to need each other. I encourage you to meet together with other women to share in the discussion questions at the end of each chapter.

I'll never forget the 70-year-old woman who participated in a group that I led over a one-week period. At the end of the week, she said, "In all my years as a Christian, I've never felt the love and support of God in the way I have this week through all of you." It was bittersweet to hear her say those words. I was glad she finally had that beautiful experience in the body of Christ, yet I was sad that it took 70 years before she felt that kind of love and support in Christian community.

My vision for this book is that it will be a tool that will bring women together to support and encourage one another. Women's ministries groups, mothers and daughters, youth groups, and neighborhood Bible studies can use this material to guide them into God's truth about a reality we all deal with. I long to see women thinking about their bodies in light of God's Word and in the context of their relationships with other women.

I feel that God has given me a commission similar to Isaiah's. Isaiah came to the people of Israel to proclaim the good news that their nation didn't have to remain in captivity to other nations. I am coming to women to proclaim that we don't have to remain in captivity to the message that our bodies aren't good enough. In fact, I think Isaiah 61:1–3 describes the beauty that God wants to bring to women:

> The Spirit of the Sovereign LORD is on me, because the LORD has anointed me to preach good news to the poor. He has sent me to bind up the brokenhearted, to proclaim freedom for the

captives and release from darkness for the prisoners, to proclaim
the year of the LORD'S favor and the day of vengeance of our
God, to comfort all who mourn, and provide for those who
grieve in Zion—to bestow on them a crown of beauty instead
of ashes, the oil of gladness instead of mourning, and a garment
of praise instead of a spirit of despair. They will be called oaks
of righteousness, a planting of the LORD for the display of his
splendor.

Isn't that what you want for yourself and the women you know?
Don't you want to exchange your ashes for beauty, your mourning for
gladness, your spirit of despair for a garment of praise? God wants that
also! So let's get started.

If You're Using This Book in a Study Group

You'll get the most out of the study group if you read the assigned
chapter before you come to the meeting, but don't skip the meeting if
you haven't had time to complete the chapter. You'll still gain valuable
insights from the other women.

I recommend that you purchase a spiral notebook or journal to
record your responses to the questions that are placed throughout the
text. A separate journal lets you keep your personal reflections private,
so you can feel free to share this book with a friend without exposing
confidential information and private thoughts. Many questions are
simply insights from Scripture, but some are more personal in nature.
Please take the time to answer each question.

I know how busy women are, and how hard it is to find time to
read and study. I've tried to make the chapters short enough that you
can read and answer the questions in under an hour. May I suggest that

you try to carve out just 10 to 15 minutes a day to read and work on the questions. That way you'll be finished with the chapter before your weekly group meeting.

The scriptures are provided in the text so that you can keep your book with you and take advantage of small blocks of time you find within your day. Of course you may choose to look up the scriptures in your own Bible so you can underline them or know where they are found. If you work outside the home, you may want to read during your lunch break. If you're a mom, you might bring your book and journal along when you take the kids to the park and study while you watch them play.

You do not need to answer the discussion questions at the end of each chapter before the meeting unless you want to. The questions don't require preparation, and will most likely be the focus of your group meeting.

Following are ground rules for a successful group discussion. Your group may have additional suggestions.

1. Everything said in the group is confidential.
2. Everything said is voluntary. You may pass if you don't want to give an answer.
3. There are no right answers. (Most answers aren't right or wrong; rather, they reflect your feelings or opinions. However, the Bible is the supreme authority.)

During the group meetings the discussion questions at the end of each chapter will be the focus of the sharing time. However, your group might sometimes wish to discuss questions from the text as well. Assume that each participant has read the chapter during the previous week. There's really no need for formal teaching; merely discuss what was read.

Above all, I hope that the study group will provide you with a sense of community. Women need to have deep connections with other women. The community becomes a place where the transformation from body loathing to body acceptance can take place. Richard Foster gave this advice for a small group he led:

> Give encouragement as often as possible; advice, once in a great while; reproof, only when absolutely necessary; and judgment, *never.*[1]

That's a good credo to use in your group. The goal of the group is to support each other in the process of allowing God to transform your lives and beliefs about who you are.

A special intimacy develops when you pray for one another. I encourage you to close each discussion time in prayer and have weekly prayer partners or a prayer list so you can pray for each person by name.

Again, let me say how delighted I am that you are participating in this study. I pray that it will lead to a life of freedom in which you are no longer plagued by the destructive power of dislike for your body. I pray that your group and individual study will be prosperous and that your soul will soar as you focus on what is really important and special about you. Always remember that every body is beautiful! Please let me know of your group's success or questions by writing me at:

Deborah Newman
Focus on the Family Author Relations
8605 Explorer Drive
Colorado Springs, CO 80920

Blessings,
Deborah Newman

CHAPTER ONE

More Than Skin Deep

⚜

aylee will never forget the day she came home from the hairdresser when she was nine years old. Her mother had wanted to curl Maylee's straight Asian hair with a perm. Unfortunately this one totally fried her hair. The hairdresser's only recourse was to cut off all the perm, leaving Maylee with a nearly-shaved head. She caught a glimpse of herself in the mirror as she left, and all she could think about was the merciless teasing she would endure.

Maylee looked like a pimply-faced boy. She had gone to the hairdresser with hopes of looking pretty, and she left feeling like a hideous freak. She ran to the car and hid under the dashboard. When she arrived home, she ran to her room, hoping that no other human being would lay eyes on her.

Maylee's mom made Maylee join her in the bathroom. She held her daughter's shoulders and forced her to stand before the mirror. She said, "Look in the mirror, Maylee. See the beautiful girl who stands there. Look at her strong, lean body. Look at her pretty brown eyes and see her nice round face. That girl is beautiful."

Maylee opened her eyes and at first saw only her awkward haircut and her blemishes. As her mother directed her, she began to notice that she did have some beauty, if she really looked. Her mother went on to sympathize with the shame and embarrassment she felt about her haircut. She said, "I know that your hair is not what we wanted it to look like. Your hair will grow out fast. I promise that we will never try to perm it again. But in spite of your haircut, you are a beautiful girl. Don't let anyone tell you anything different."

My weight bothers me each and every day;
even every minute of every day.

Her mom's words fortified a place deep in Maylee's soul that day. She remembers that lesson from the mirror more than she remembers the shame and teasing she experienced while her hair grew out. You see, focusing on the truth and getting the right perspective from her mom created deep self-confidence that helps Maylee even today to fight the kind of body disgrace that plagues others.

In the same way, God asks you to stand before the mirror with Him by your side. He wants to show you the beauty that He intended, the beauty you overlook. He wants to acknowledge the parts of you that are unappreciated by the culture you live in. He gives you the same advice Maylee's mother gave her. He shows you that indeed you are beautiful.

In my experience as a counselor and now as a minister to women, I have discovered that the only true healing for body-image issues is a spiritual healing. This book is intended to present you with God's words about your body. When His Word pierces your soul (Hebrews

4:12), it inoculates you from the shouts, whispers, and inferences that your body is not good enough.

What is it you most dislike about yourself? I want you to mention only one thing. I know it won't take you long to answer this question: "If you could change one thing about your body, what would it be?" Turn to your journal or notebook and write down your answer. Now I invite you to offer to God that one thing you mentioned for His healing. Pray this prayer as you begin this study:

> Dear heavenly Father,
> I want to ask you right now to help me receive Your truth
> about my body. I offer my _____ (body part I most want to
> change) to You. Help me see the truth about why You gave me
> this body. I invite You to fill me with Your Holy Spirit. Let
> Your Word bring healing from a negative body image. Help me
> become an agent of truth regarding body image in my world.
> In Jesus' name. Amen.

Why Don't We Like Ourselves?

We overemphasize how we look. We succumb to expensive and even life-threatening measures to look good. While a man may wear a hairpiece, put shoulder pads in his coat, or wear elevated shoes, women are more likely to have cosmetic surgery, starve, or throw up. Some women literally put their lives at risk for the sake of beauty.

This is not just a twenty-first-century problem. For generations women have been body haters. Think of the corsets women wore in Civil War times. And did you know that during the Elizabethan era some women would actually take a little arsenic to achieve the pale appearance that was considered beautiful at that time?

How did we get this way? Many believe that women have achieved power through the ages because of their beauty and sexual attractiveness. For example, one of the best-known Egyptian queens, Cleopatra, rose to power because of her sensuality, which gave her influence over the men who ruled the world.

Though the problem of women disliking their bodies is nothing new, the number of victims is on the increase. Some blame the media, which plaster perfectly shaped and toned women in our faces constantly. Others say it's the outright sinful preoccupation we have with ourselves. Whatever the reason, we can be certain that negative body image is impoverishing the lives of women and girls across our nation and certain other parts of the world. Let's look at a few statistics:

- Americans had 10.2 million plastic surgery procedures in 2005, up 11 percent from 2004.[1]
- More than half of teenage girls are, or think they should be, on diets. They want to lose some or all of the 40 pounds that females naturally gain between ages 8 and 14. About 3 percent of these teens go too far, becoming anorexic or bulimic.[2]
- The *Medical Journal of Psychiatry* conducted a general population study on men with eating disorders and found that 2 percent of men, compared to 4.8 percent of women, have anorexia or bulimia.[3]
- The average American woman is five feet four inches tall and weighs 140 pounds, while the average American model is five feet 11 inches tall and weighs 117 pounds. Most fashion models are thinner than 98 percent of American women.[4]
- Eighty percent of American women are dissatisfied with their appearance.[5]
- Female athletes are six times more likely to develop eating disorders than are other women.[6]

- Eighty percent of women say that the images of women on television and in movies, fashion magazines, and advertising make them feel insecure.[7]
- Forty-two percent of girls in first through third grades want to be thinner.[8]
- Eighty-one percent of 10-year-olds are afraid of being fat.[9]
- Without treatment, up to 20 percent of people with serious eating disorders die. With treatment, that number falls to 2 to 3 percent.[10]
- The average woman spends two and a half years of her life washing, styling, cutting, coloring, crimping, and straightening her hair at home and in the salon.[11]

I doubt that you can think of 10 women among your acquaintances who would say they are very satisfied with their appearance.

The Bride of Solomon Was Not Comfortable in Her Own Skin

Even the bride of Solomon had a poor body image. She lamented, "Do not stare at me because I am dark, because I am darkened by the sun. My mother's sons were angry with me and made me take care of the vineyards; my own vineyard I have neglected" (Song of Songs 1:6).

🌷 How did she feel about her body? (Remember to write your answer in your journal.)

She hated her dark skin. Today many Caucasians are literally dying (from skin cancer) to be tan. This raises a fundamental point: Body image is more about what's in our heads than how we look on the outside. For example, I could look in the mirror and think I look great, then notice an hour later that I had a piece of lettuce stuck between my teeth. For an hour, I thought I looked great because my feeling was based on subjective information—what I thought I looked like, rather than objective information—what I actually looked like.

Now let's look at Song of Songs 2:1: "I am a rose of Sharon, a lily of the valleys."

꿏 How does the bride of Solomon feel about her body now? What caused the change?

This woman's body image has unmistakably been transformed. She could be the poster child for being comfortable in your own skin. Now she is calling herself a rose of Sharon and a lily of the valleys. Her dark skin didn't change; she didn't have bleaching techniques in those days to get skin the "right" shade. What changed was her thinking: She began to believe she was beautiful.

Yes, she had a man in her life who thought she was absolutely amazing. (You can read chapter 1 of Song of Songs and see why.) But some women reading this book are in relationships with men who constantly put them down for their weight or other body flaws. If that's your situation, you will need extra support and prayers as you begin to see yourself truthfully.

However, most men, like King Solomon, don't notice the body issues women get so stuck on. Most of the men in our lives would love for us to accept ourselves and be free of body loathing. I want to assure you that the spiritual transformation I'm talking about can happen with or without the support of a man.

I'm praying that you will have the same transformation as the bride of Solomon. A cosmetic surgeon will never get these kinds of results. Only God can reach the part of a woman that needs His healing touch.

If you are willing, you can find out what it feels like to be comfortable in your own skin.

*I'm afraid to let anyone
see me without makeup.*

When it comes to changing our body image, we don't rely on objective data. Remember Susan, the 16-year-old who hated her arms? If she could focus on objective data, she would have many reasons to feel attractive. At five feet four inches in a size 9, she is not overweight. She is fit. She has developed muscle mass through her weekly drill-team workouts. She is an example of prime teenage fitness, even though all of that is at risk if she follows through on the self-destructive path of bulimia.

The reason Susan can't look at herself and appreciate these objective realities isn't because her mirror is distorted. Her body image has little to do with how she looks on the outside, but everything to do with what she thinks and feels on the inside.

Let's look at the objective data about Susan:

Age: 16
Height: 5'4"
Weight: 125 pounds
Size: 9
Hair: shoulder length, naturally blonde with a slight wave
Fitness routine: works out 10 hours a week with the
        dance/drill team

Would you say:

_____ she's just right.
_____ she's a little too fat.

_____ she needs to exercise more.

_____ she overdoes the exercise, but probably looks nice anyway.

_____ I can understand why she doesn't feel attractive enough because a size 9 is a little big.

❦ Why do you think this way?

Read the objective data about Marybeth (the woman who refused to be in the fashion show):

Age: 49

Height: 5'6"

Weight: 150

Size: 12

Hair: short, highlighted, layered

Fitness routine: swims three times a week at the Y

Would you say:

_____ she's just right.

_____ she's a little too fat.

_____ she needs to exercise more.

_____ she overdoes exercise, but looks good anyway.

_____ I can understand why she doesn't feel good about herself because size 12 is a little big.

❦ Why do you think this way?

If you are participating in a discussion group, you will probably find that there are different opinions about Susan's and Marybeth's objective information. Let's consider what influenced you to develop your opinion about your body and others' bodies.

What Is Body Image?

You develop your body image slowly without stopping to think about it. You flip through magazines, watch television, and hear comments about your body from your mother, father, siblings, boyfriend or husband, coaches, and others. As you compare yourself with other women, you are developing your body image. Subtle beliefs get into your mind, such as, *My thighs shouldn't touch, my stomach must be flat, and my arms can't wag!* All these negative thoughts can lead you on a self-destructive path if you don't recognize them as unrealistic and false.

Susan can remember actually liking herself when she was in fourth grade. She was a fast runner and one day she even beat Tim Hill in a race during PE. She loved to get a new Easter dress each year and felt pretty when she joined her family at church. She used to get so many compliments about her naturally curly hair that it was embarrassing.

I wish my nose was symmetrical.

It wasn't until sixth grade that Susan started to worry about her body. That summer at camp, her counselor skipped dessert and ritualistically performed 130 sit-ups every night. Susan's girlfriends at school, who had once avoided boys like the plague, now based their worth and dignity on whether guys liked them.

Susan didn't like boys the same way her friends did, but she felt pressure to have a boyfriend. When the guy she chose, Andrew, told his friend, who told Susan's friend that he liked her back, she felt exhilarated. But when Andrew made fun of her wobbly thighs, she felt crushed. That's the first time Susan remembers disliking her body.

Marybeth had to think hard about when she had ever liked her body. She couldn't remember a time. It wasn't because she was older and her memory was fading. She literally began hating her body when she was four years old and her stepfather started molesting her. She both hated and loved the man who hurt her, but she only hated the body to which it happened. In her four-year-old mind she reasoned, *There must be something wrong with me for him to treat me this way.*

You would think with that kind of body hate Marybeth would have ignored her body and never tried to look good. Actually, the opposite was true. She spent her time trying to make herself look good enough, but in her mind she never succeeded. She continually kept up with the latest fashions, and although she didn't dress seductively or extravagantly, she was an expert in gaining approval for how she dressed. It's just that the approval was never accepted—it bounced right off her.

I feel like I would lose everything—my husband,
my friends, my life—if I gained one pound.

Christine, the woman who took Marybeth's place in the fashion show, has many painful memories from her childhood about being overweight. She dreaded the change of seasons because it meant one thing—shopping for new clothes with Mom. She remembers the embarrassment she felt as her mom dragged her from store to store asking if they carried half sizes.

Christine started her first diet in third grade. She desperately wanted to please her mom, but she never succeeded. In fact, just last year she realized that the yo-yo diets she had been on all her life were attempts to make her mother accept and like her.

Ironically, when Christine turned 30, she and her mom wore the same dress size, and her mother finally accepted Christine and loved to shop for her. Having her mother's approval wasn't the answer to Christine's self-rejection, though. Her body image changed when she finally let God's opinion of her body be the one that mattered. The new exercise plan she is starting is the first time she has ever done anything positive for her body for the right reason. She is attempting to take care of the body God gave her, rather than trying to get her mom's approval or fit into a size 8.

You may be thinking, *I can see how a negative body image could develop from being subjected to the kind of sexual trauma Marybeth went through, but why would I have cause to hate myself?* That's what I want you to think about in this next exercise—your own life experiences. I'll ask you to write down memories you have of yourself at different life stages. Perhaps you've never consciously thought about why you dislike the reflection in the mirror. It is important that you become conscious of exactly what is driving your dissatisfaction with your body in order to overcome it.

This may be a very difficult exercise for you. Most of us try to avoid these painful memories. You will have to trust me that stirring them up will be good for you in the end. As you write, you may feel pain; you may even cry. On the other hand, if you have hardened yourself, you may not feel anything. In either case, it is important that you attempt to survey memories you have of your body during these life stages. We'll work on how to resolve your feelings (or get in touch with your feelings) in future chapters.

As you answer the following questions, try to picture yourself and how you looked at the time. If you have photos of yourself at each stage, they will aid you in remembering how you felt. Leave some blank space in your journal after each stage of development. As you read this book, you may have more memories that you will want to record in the blank spaces.

I encourage you to ask God to help you remember any painful experiences so that you can receive healing. Now let's get started on the exercise.

Body History Reflection: A Chronological Survey

As you read through the stages below, think back to how you felt about your body, and write down memories you have of those particular stages of development. Pay special attention to recalling specific statements people made about your body or their bodies. For example, "My mom told me that after I was born, she gained 60 pounds." "My father told me he felt sorry for me because my skin was too dark."

I've discovered that sometimes body-image problems are linked to unintentional messages children received while undergoing medical procedures that they didn't understand. I will ask you whether you experienced any unusual medical procedures during your childhood and to consider any negative messages you may have received.

Stage One: Preschool Years, Ages 0–6
- How did your parents react to your body size?
- How did your parents care for your bodily and emotional needs?
- How did you discover that you were different from males? Did you undergo any major medical procedures?
- How much did your parents or caregivers focus on their weight or fitness?
- Do you remember a feeling of being comfortable in your own skin at this stage of life?
- When you think about your body at these ages, what do you remember feeling?

Stage Two: School-Age Years, Grades 1–4
- How did you relate to peers?
- Were you called names or teased?
- Did you have friends?
- How did you feel about your performance at school?
- Did you undergo any major medical procedures?
- How did you feel about the opposite sex?
- Did you experience any physical, sexual, mental, or emotional abuse?
- How did you feel about yourself in a bathing suit?
- How did your mother react to her body?

Stage Three: Puberty Years, Grades 5–8
- How did your friends talk about their bodies or your body? What did you think of your developing body?
- How did you feel about the onset of menstruation?
- Did you know it's normal for girls to gain 20–40 pounds at this age?
- Did your parents and siblings accept your body?
- Did you undergo any medical procedures that affected the way you felt toward your body?
- What did you like or dislike about your body?

Stage Four: High School Years, Grades 9–12
- Were you the subject of teasing?
- How were you treated by the opposite sex?
- Did you think your body size or looks had an impact on dating?
- How did you handle peer pressure regarding sex, drugs, and drinking?

- Did you feel accepted by a group at school?
- How did your teachers treat you?
- Did you experience any unwanted sexual advances?
- How did you feel about being in a bathing suit?

Stage Five: Young Adult Years, Ages 18–29
- Did you feel your appearance had an impact on your vocation, dating, or marriage?
- How did you think of your body on significant birthdays? How did you feel about yourself in a bathing suit?
- How did you feel about your body on your wedding day? How did you feel about your body during or after pregnancy?
- Were there any life events (divorce, job loss, and so on) that caused you to dislike your body or blame the way you look?

Stage Six: Adult Years, Ages 30–55
- Use some of the questions from above.
- How did you feel about your changing metabolism, gray hair, wrinkles?

Stage Seven: Senior Adult Years, 55+
- Use some of the questions from above.
- Have major health issues affected how you see your body?
- How have you adjusted to changes related to aging?

🌱 In doing the exercise above, did you discover any experiences that may have contributed to your poor body image?

We will come back to these memories in later chapters. For now, it is good that you are starting to consider why you feel the way you do about your body. Keep praying and asking God to reveal any hurt that you are harboring and need His healing for. As other memories come to mind, write them down in this section of your journal.

What Is a Healthy Body Image?

Of the three women we've just talked about, Christine is the one with the healthiest body image. Yet, in the world's view she would be considered the least attractive because she is overweight. Why does she have a healthy body image? Read about what a healthy body image is, and you will better understand.

A healthy body image is characterized by three major components: respect, care, and perspective. A woman with a healthy body image respects her body, takes care of her body, and keeps her body in perspective.

A Healthy Body Image Involves Respect

In Psalm 139:13–16 David is referring to his body:

> For you created my inmost being; you knit me together in my mother's womb. I praise you because I am fearfully and wonderfully made; your works are wonderful, I know that full well. My frame was not hidden from you when I was made in the secret place. When I was woven together in the depths of the earth, your eyes saw my unformed body. All the days ordained for me were written in your book before one of them came to be.

🌱 Why is David in awe of his body?

🌱 Have you ever pondered your body in the same way?

❦ Write a psalm to God telling Him why you are in awe of the way you were made.

A healthy body image involves a sense of respect for the miracle your body is. According to Romans 1:20, the reality that there is a God who designed the universe is all around us every day: "For since the creation of the world God's invisible qualities—his eternal power and divine nature—have been clearly seen, being understood from what has been made, so that men are without excuse." Even if your body has been handicapped, it is still a miraculous testimony of God our Creator.

Do you realize that numerous organs, blood vessels, muscles, and bones are involved when you just move your index finger up and down? A person with a healthy body image respects the reality that God gave her a body as a gift. Others may not think the way you look is "all that," but God created you, and to Him you are "all that" and more! If you have a healthy body image, you will respect that you are fearfully and wonderfully made by a caring and loving God who has a plan for your life. If you feel ugly and poorly made, you have an unhealthy body image.

❦ Check yourself:

_____ I know I have body flaws, but I recognize God made me the way I am.

_____ I still don't accept how I look.

A Healthy Body Image Involves Care

Satan knows that we look out for our bodies. In Job 2, after Satan had destroyed all of Job's material possessions and children, Satan approached God and the two had this conversation:

Then the LORD said to Satan, "Have you considered my servant Job? There is no one on earth like him; he is blameless and upright, a man who fears God and shuns evil. And he still maintains his integrity, though you incited me against him to ruin him without any reason."

"Skin for skin!" Satan replied. "A man will give all he has for his own life. But stretch out your hand and strike his flesh and bones, and he will surely curse you to your face." (Job 2:3–5)

🌱 What was Satan's excuse for why Job had not given up on God?

🌱 Do you have a natural desire to protect your body from harm?

Satan knows that our natural, healthy instincts are to care for our bodies. When we are thinking of our bodies correctly, we won't allow harm to come to them. We will eat well, and we will get proper exercise and rest. We won't overwork ourselves to the point of exhaustion.

Are you doing anything to your body to harm it? Do you care for your body correctly? If you are not taking care of your body, you do not have a healthy body image.

🌱 Check yourself:

_____ I eat right, and get some exercise and proper rest. I don't overwork my body.

_____ I don't follow the advice I know is best about how to eat and exercise.

A Healthy Body Image Involves Perspective

In 2 Corinthians 10:12, Paul speaks of the futility of comparing ourselves to others: "We do not dare to classify or compare ourselves with
some who commend themselves. When they measure themselves by
themselves and compare themselves with themselves, they are not wise."

> ᛉ Is it foolish to compare our physical attributes with others?
> Why or why not?

The world measures men and women by their looks, their talents,
their money, and their power. God has a completely different appraisal
system. We aren't supposed to measure ourselves by other people. We
should measure ourselves only by God's Word. The following passage
from 1 Corinthians is referring to the work of the kingdom, but it
could also apply to our physical attributes.

> And in the church God has appointed first of all apostles, sec-
> ond prophets, third teachers, then workers of miracles, also
> those having gifts of healing, those able to help others, those
> with gifts of administration, and those speaking in different
> kinds of tongues. Are all apostles? Are all prophets? Are all
> teachers? Do all work miracles? Do all have gifts of healing? Do
> all speak in tongues? Do all interpret? (1 Corinthians 12:28–30)

> ᛉ How can your physical attributes affect the work God has
> given you to do in the kingdom?

> ᛉ Do you think you need to have certain physical attributes or
> personality attributes to serve in the kingdom?

🌱 If someone has "nicer" attributes than you, how should you feel about that person? About yourself?

God didn't create all of us to fit the latest concept of beautiful. We define beauty by our specific culture in a specific time. Many famous beauties of past centuries are not considered beautiful today. Marilyn Monroe, a beauty icon of the 1950s, would be considered overweight in our culture. Many beauties of today may not be considered beautiful in the future.

Look at how God created people. He created variety. He made different shades of skin color, a variety of eye and hair colors. People are a rainbow of beauty in the eyes of the Creator. It's our differences that make us beautiful. If you can't see the unique beauty in yourself and others, then you don't have a healthy body image.

🌱 Check yourself:

_____ I can see beauty in myself and others. I don't define beauty by comparison to runway models.

_____ I feel jealous when I see others who are more attractive than I am.

One of the most profound quotes I use to explain healthy body image is about spiritual truth, but it applies beautifully to the place where I long for you to arrive. George MacDonald said, "I would rather be what God chose to make me than the most glorious creature that I could think of; for to have been thought about, born in God's thought, and then made by God, is the dearest, grandest and most precious thing in all thinking."[12] I'm hoping that you will be able to make this same bold proclamation about living in your own skin.

Discussion Questions

1. Have you ever felt uncomfortable with the way you look as the bride of Solomon did in Song of Songs 1:6? Why do you think women obsess over their body flaws rather than enjoy the things that are right with their bodies?

2. What changed for the bride of Solomon so that she felt comfortable enough to call herself a rose of Sharon in Song of Songs 2:1? Did her skin color change?

3. Go around the room and share the most attractive physical characteristic (eyes, height, nose, hair, etc.) of the person on your right.

4. Go around the room and share the most positive character quality (kindness, generosity, thoughtfulness, etc.) of the person on your left.

5. Go around the room and state the physical characteristic you like best about yourself and thank God for it; for example, "Thank You, God, that You gave me big brown eyes."

6. How do you think God wants us to think about our bodies based on the information in Psalm 139:15–16? (God knows our frame. He oversaw our creation. God knows how long we will live in these bodies while on earth. Before we ever saw ourselves, He knew it all!)

CHAPTER TWO

A World Without Beauty

❦

*I*magine a world where everyone looked like Barbie and Ken dolls. Picture an entire group of people you interact with daily (males and females) looking this way. (You could choose your work group, a class at school, a small group from church, or your family, for example.) How do you think people would interact if every single person in that group looked like either Ken or Barbie? In your mind give the Barbies and Kens the personalities of people you know. Imagine all the Kens dressed in the same outfit and all the Barbies dressed in the same outfit.

Try to imagine yourself as a Barbie, talking to the other Barbies and Kens. Would you finally like yourself? Would you think you were as pretty as the other Barbies, whom you look exactly like? Would you be envious of the other Barbies? Would you think they were envious of you? Would everyone in the group be happy with how they looked? Would anyone be depressed? Would anyone struggle with body image? Would anyone feel better than everyone else based on how he or she looked?

Does this exercise conjure up images of a sci-fi movie? It's such an unreal and bizarre concept that you may find it hard to even think in this way. Try anyway. Think of how these people would interact if they all looked the same. It wouldn't take long for the individuals to find a way to look different from the rest of the group. The girls who needed to think of themselves as better than the others would do their hair in a different way to try to validate their importance. Each person would pierce and tattoo, cut and shave—anything to look unique and different.

I wish I had bigger lips.

If we all looked exactly the same, our inner imperfections would turn up in other ways. Perfection isn't achieved through having flat abs or firm breasts. In fact, you can never achieve perfection when it comes to your body. So why is beauty such a big illusion?

Some would blame Barbie herself for creating the illusion of perfection. Let's face it, Barbie is a total fantasy. Have you seen the statistics that demonstrate how impossible it would be for Barbie to exist in human form? "Exceptionally tall, but with a child's size-three foot permanently molded in a high-heeled position, Barbie's measurements read 39-18-33."[1]

Now let's see how much perfectionism influences your thinking. Answer each question below true or false.

Perfection Scale

_____ Beautiful people have the best of life.

_____ I know that if people saw me before I fixed myself up, they wouldn't like me at all.

_____ People will notice and think poorly of me if I have a blemish on my face.

_____ How people look reflects how valuable they are to society.

_____ If I eat cake (or other sweets) I will feel fat.

_____ The way I look is a big reason why I haven't achieved what I've wanted to in life.

_____ The only way I could ever be happy with the way I look is if I could change several of my physical characteristics.

_____ I believe I can make my appearance what I want it to be if I spend a lot of money on the right kinds of beauty products and procedures.

_____ If I can just look the right way, then I can have the relationships, job, joy, and peace that I want.

_____ I am ashamed of how I look.

Total number of true statements: _____

0	No perfectionism
1–2	Mild perfectionism
3–7	Moderate perfectionism
8–10	Severe perfectionism

Every one of these statements expresses perfection. They represent many of the wrong assumptions that affect our body images negatively. The more true responses you have, the more you need to recognize the dangerous and suffocating problem of negative body image. Perhaps it's time to think about what fuels your perfectionism about your body, so you can learn to break free from its hold.

I believe the illusion and the quest for perfection have a history far older and deeper than Barbie dolls and modern culture. The problem of body image goes back to the time before the first man and woman were created. The true roots of a poor body image are found in the creator of lies, Satan himself (John 8:44). Let's expose Satan's involvement in beauty and deceit. It will help you understand the larger spiritual war you are involved in.

We know a lot about Satan and his work on earth. He claims every unsaved soul as his own; he is not only the father of lies, but he was a murderer from the beginning (John 8:44); he is the god of this age (2 Corinthians 4:4); he distorts God's Word (Genesis 3); and he is always seeking someone to devour (1 Peter 5:8). He fell into sin through beauty and deceit, and he uses those same tactics to trap souls today. Ezekiel 28:11–19 describes Satan this way:

> The word of the LORD came to me: "Son of man, take up a
> lament concerning the king of Tyre and say to him: 'This is
> what the Sovereign LORD says: You were the model of perfec-
> tion, full of wisdom and perfect in beauty. You were in Eden,
> the garden of God; every precious stone adorned you: ruby,
> topaz and emerald, chrysolite, onyx and jasper, sapphire,
> turquoise and beryl. Your settings and mountings were made
> of gold; on the day you were created they were prepared. You
> were anointed as a guardian cherub, for so I ordained you. You
> were on the holy mount of God; you walked among the fiery
> stones. You were blameless in your ways from the day you were
> created till wickedness was found in you. Through your wide-
> spread trade you were filled with violence, and you sinned. So
> I drove you in disgrace from the mount of God, and I expelled
> you, O guardian cherub, from among the fiery stones. Your
> heart became proud on account of your beauty, and you cor-
> rupted your wisdom because of your splendor. So I threw you
> to the earth; I made a spectacle of you before kings. By your

many sins and dishonest trade you have desecrated your sanc-
tuaries. So I made a fire come out from you, and it consumed
you, and I reduced you to ashes on the ground in the sight of
all who were watching. All the nations who knew you are
appalled at you; you have come to a horrible end and will be
no more.' "

❦ What did Satan look like when God created him?

God created Satan in awesome beauty and splendor. He was the
model of perfection—the measuring stick for what is beautiful in
God's creation. Nowhere in the rest of creation could there be found a
being that could compare to the beauty he possessed. This passage is
conveying that if a heavenly beauty pageant had been held, Satan
would have won hands down.

God didn't make Satan just beautiful, though; He also made him
wise. It would have been unfair of God to give him that kind of beauty
without the wisdom to go along with it. Without wisdom he might
have had an excuse for desiring to exalt himself above God. But
although Satan did possess wisdom, he didn't use it to glorify God.

❦ Why did Satan turn away from God? (See Ezekiel 28:11–19
above.)

It was Satan's beauty that first turned his heart to wickedness. It
made his heart proud, and that pride corrupted his wisdom. Where
once his beauty glorified the Creator who had granted such wonder,
now his beauty made him think he could glorify himself even more
through his own effort. His corrupt wisdom told him that he could
become more by taking over God's kingdom.

⚡ What will happen to Satan in the end? (See Ezekiel 28:11–19 above.)

This passage is one of the many prophesies about Satan's desperate destiny. Although once he walked on the fiery stones, there will come a day when he will be consumed by fire. Many will be looking at him then, but they won't be admiring his beauty. They will be appalled at him instead.

Now let's look at Genesis 3:14–15:

So the LORD God said to the serpent, "Because you have done this, cursed are you above all the livestock and all the wild animals! You will crawl on your belly and you will eat dust all the days of your life. And I will put enmity between you and the woman, and between your offspring and hers; he will crush your head, and you will strike his heel."

⚡ What did the serpent look like when God cursed him?

Evidently, after Satan sinned and was cast down to earth, he still desired to use wisdom and beauty for influence. When he came as an animal to tempt Adam and Eve, he chose the form of a serpent, the craftiest of all the wild animals. When God judged the serpent, He made it the lowliest and most dreaded of all the creatures. God made the serpent crawl on his belly and eat dust all his existence on earth.

This is a picture of what had already happened to Satan. Although he can disguise himself as an angel of light (2 Corinthians 11:14), he has lost all the beauty that once adorned his very being. It's also a picture of our redemption through Jesus Christ. The seed of woman

(Christ) would crush his head, and the serpent would strike His heel. On the cross Jesus' heel was struck, but at the Resurrection Satan's head was crushed!

Let's look at another passage that can be applied to Satan, Isaiah 14:11–15:

> All your pomp has been brought down to the grave, along with the noise of your harps; maggots are spread out beneath you and worms cover you. How you have fallen from heaven, O morning star, son of the dawn! You have been cast down to the earth, you who once laid low the nations! You said in your heart, "I will ascend to heaven; I will raise my throne above the stars of God; I will sit enthroned on the mount of assembly, on the utmost heights of the sacred mountain. I will ascend above the tops of the clouds; I will make myself like the Most High." But you are brought down to the grave, to the depths of the pit.

❦ How do these verses describe Satan?

Satan has lost all of his pomp in his present condition. He was once a bright and morning star in heaven, but he will eventually be cast down to the grave with maggots and worms. Satan isn't there yet, but a day and time are coming when God will make good on His promises.

❦ What were the five "I will" statements that Satan made?

Let's compare Satan's attitude as expressed in the five "I will" statements with an attitude of humble submission to God.

Satan's attitude:	An attitude of humble submission:
1. I will ascend to heaven.	I will recognize God's loving, ruling power in my life.
2. I will raise my throne above the stars of God.	I will keep God on the throne and bow down from mine.
3. I will sit enthroned on the mount of the assembly.	I will worship with the others in the assembly.
4. I will ascend above the tops of the clouds.	I will let God lift me up in His time.
5. I will make myself like the Most High.	I will serve God faithfully.

❦ How do you think having a poor body image compares with trying to make yourself like God?

I believe poor body image has its roots far deeper than advertising and cultural influences (although I do agree, those influences are powerful). I believe that poor body image has close connections to original sin, by way of the originator of sin, Satan himself. The spiritual root of all body image struggles is doubting God's goodness in the way He made you. I don't know anyone who struggles with a poor body image who would say that she is trying to be beautiful so she can worship God fully. I do know that every human sinner desires to be accepted, to be better than others, and to stand out. This is the problem at the root of all body loathing that fills the earth.

There is nothing Satan would enjoy more than getting women to feel ugly and useless. Pursuing perfectionist dreams will ultimately lead you to a world with distorted beauty just as it did for him. Let's learn from Satan's wicked example and move away from being consumed by beauty and perfectionism. It will require putting your faith and trust in the power of Jesus Christ working through you.

> *My husband is attracted to thin women*
> *who appear to have breast implants,*
> *yet he says he would never want me to do*
> *that to my body. It's hard for me to believe*
> *that I am attractive to him.*

How Do We Lose Touch with Our True Beauty?

Body image has little to do with how you actually look. Body image is what you think you look like on the outside. As a result, it changes from day to day. For example, Karen is the prettiest woman in her circle of friends. When she is out to lunch with them and around town, she never struggles with her body image. She thinks she looks good and goes on with her life with little concern about how she looks.

> *Even though a part of me knows I am attractive*
> *and I get whistled at on the street, deep inside I*
> *still feel like the fat 10-year-old that no one*
> *thought was anything special.*

But when someone enters her world who is prettier than she is, she's flooded with insecurity. Suddenly the 10 pounds she has gained become an inner tube around her stomach, and she feels like the ugliest woman in the world.

Like Karen, physical comparisons go through your mind every day. You aren't always aware of them and how they affect you. Other subtle toxins you may not be aware of have damaged your sense of self. In chapter one, you took a chronological overview of how you felt about your body. The following exercise will help you further identify those subtle toxins that are polluting your ability to see your true beauty.

Name Exercise

1. In your journal, write down any names that others called you from your childhood to the present. Include names, whether positive or negative, that described your body or other characteristics attributed to you.
2. If this name exercise brings up memories you haven't written in your chronological survey, record them there also.
3. Out of obedience to Christ and your desire to fully receive God's healing, go over your list and mark out any negative names you were called.
4. Write 1 John 3:1 across the bottom of your page: "How great is the love the Father has lavished on us, that we should be called children of God! And that is what we are!" Underneath the scripture write out the statement, "I will be called ____ (your first name), God's daughter. From now on, I will not answer to any other name."

Where Did Your Beauty Go?

It's critical for you to acknowledge how often your negative body image has been reinforced over your lifetime. When a statement is reinforced over and over, it takes on a sense of truth, even if it is not true. Negative feelings, experiences, and comments combine into a powerful force that blinds you from seeing who you really are.

When I help others work through a negative body-image problem, I start with two questions. The first is, "What do you most dislike about your body?" You already answered that question in chapter one. The chronological survey and name exercise have helped you answer the second question: "When do you remember first not liking that part of you?" Answer these two questions in your journal.

You Can Overcome a Negative Body Image

Do you identify any consistencies between your chronological survey in chapter one and the part of your body that you dislike most? For instance, Susan, the 16-year-old bulimic, said her most positive feature was her brown eyes, and most negative, her big bottom. When she compared that to what she wrote in her chronological survey in chapter one, she remembered how her dad used to sing to her about her big brown eyes, and how guys in the cafeteria put girls down the most about their behinds. For Susan there was a direct correlation.

As you look back over your responses, the impact of your experiences on your body image will become more obvious to you. The more negative your experiences with your body have been, the more self- and body-rejecting you are. But you do not have to be imprisoned by these experiences. In fact, just bringing them into your conscious awareness gives you power over them and their negative influence on how you see yourself.

Personally, I didn't think much about my body until I was about 12 or 13. Before then, I was frustrated that I couldn't do a cartwheel, but proud that I could swim three lengths of my pool in one breath.

Suddenly, something happened. I grew taller. I had always been painfully thin. But when I was 13, thin was in. I began getting attention from older guys at my school. Many people commented that I could be a model.

I don't have eyebrows or eyelashes that you can see. I use makeup to look better, but I wish I could be normal.

But then there were the other comments. I didn't develop in the breast area. This became open opportunity for painful comments. In spite of that, I discovered a new avenue to gaining approval as a female. I found that if I looked good—if I enhanced my appearance with makeup and clothes—I could ward off unwanted rejection and receive approval.

Then in the midst of my early adolescence, when I wasn't even seeking God, He showed me a secret that kept me a little more sane and less depressed than many of the girls I meet these days. It is the secret to true beauty.

I distinctly remember being 14 years old and looking in a magazine while dreaming of modeling someday. As I turned the pages of that magazine, the reality of how many beautiful people there are in the world overwhelmed me. I thought to myself, *I could never be the prettiest; I'd better develop some other qualities.* At that time I wasn't listening to God's voice in my life. I was a Christian, but out of touch with God. Now I know it was God who was showing me where true beauty can be found.

We are fooling ourselves if we believe having the perfect looks will make us happy inside. Some of the world's most beautiful people are the ones most torn by heartache, broken relationships, and even poor body image. The secret to true beauty is being at peace with who you are.

God gave me another perspective on how He might have protected me because of my body flaws. I must admit, I'm thankful for my small breasts. Between the ages of 13 and 15 I began to receive a lot of attention from boys. Knowing how far I was then from yielding to God's direction for my life, I realize that feeling negatively about that part of my body actually helped me not get in trouble sexually. If I had felt more confident about how sexy I was, I might have compromised even more in my rebellion during those years.

I must admit too, that as a mother of teens, I still feel the pressure to look good. It's not as extreme as it is for those who are 12 to 21, but it's there. I have thoughts that my stomach is too round, my breasts are too small. However, I refuse to worry about my arms wagging in the wind! When I find myself succumbing, I remember that the secret to overcoming a negative body image is letting God show me my true beauty. Believe me, it's great to know the pressure to look good doesn't have to rule my life. Celebrating rather than debasing my body is a wonderful way to live.

Coming Back to Beauty

Bruce Springsteen wrote, "It's a sad man, my friend, who is living in his own skin, but can't stand the company."[2] Self-loathing comes naturally. It is a part of Satan's grasp on you. Self-acceptance is supernatural; it requires God's grace. When you begin to get God's perspective on your body and deny the messages that drive you to dislike yourself, you will find yourself loving your body for the right reasons.

The source of all your self-loathing is your own fear of being rejected by others as much as you reject yourself. Rejecting yourself takes up a great deal of time and energy. Now I would like you to take inventory of how much energy you spend avoiding your own or others' rejection. The three questions below will help you take an honest look at how much time you spend trying to get your body to be what you think it should be.

Finding the Energy to Heal

1. How much time do you spend each day working on your body—applying makeup, exercising, fixing your hair, dressing, and so on?
2. How much time do you spend each month? Multiply your daily time, and add nail appointments, shopping for clothes and beauty products, hairdresser appointments, and so on.
3. How much time do you spend per day thinking about, examining, and fantasizing about fixing your body flaws?

Exercising three times a week helps increase my totals to 30 hours a month. If your exercise isn't excessive, then that is a good reason to spend time on your body; it does take time to exercise properly. If your beauty routines require more than 40 hours per month, you probably should think about why you commit so much time to beauty. Are you in bondage to fear of rejection?

Callie couldn't stand the size of her arms. She thought they revealed to the world a secret she could keep with the right clothes: that she really was a fat nobody. She had spent days shopping for a prom dress with sleeves or a wrap that could disguise her disgrace. She found nothing. Callie just rolled her eyes when I challenged her to wear the sleeveless dress she liked to the prom. To her, I was an out-of-touch, middle-aged woman who didn't understand what was really important in the life of a 17-year-old.

No one could convince her that her arms looked fine. There was no way she would be free to have fun at her prom. She was consumed with frustration, hatred, and bad feelings. Her negative thoughts drained her of the energy to enjoy living.

I have more freckles than anyone I know.

Callie's totals ended up being 60 hours per month, plus the time she spent incessantly thinking about her body flaws. Something had to give. She longed to find a dress that she could feel good about when she went to her prom. She wanted peace, but she was caught in a trap of self-loathing.

Callie and I discussed the emotional trap that had clamped down on her arms. We compared it to the kind of traps hunters use to catch wild animals. The more she struggled with her hate of her arms, the deeper the trap pressed into her flesh and held her back.

I asked, "How do you get out of a trap like that?" Callie realized that the solution was to stop focusing on her arms. If she were caught in a trap, she would look for a way to open the hinge. The hinge to the trap of body hate was to learn how to love her body in a healthy way. Callie didn't need to spend more time trying to make her body better. She needed to make time to accept the body God blessed her with.

I was always the brunt of schoolboy comments.
They tore me apart from my hair to my big rear.
I'm 45, but I still carry their brutal pronounce-
ments with me every day.

Callie chose two of the suggested exercises below to help her fight her natural tendency to hate herself. Even though she didn't believe they would help much, she did them because at least they would interrupt the amount of time and energy she spent berating herself. She was kind to herself by taking a bubble bath and by taking her dog for a half-hour walk while thanking God for her body. These exercises weren't an instant fix, but they did stop her hopelessness for a period of time. They diverted her from her arm obsession.

Choose one or more of the following exercises to do this week.

1. Sit on a bench at a mall and find positive physical features about everyone who walks by.
2. Start a list of things you can do with your body. (I can play the violin. I can hike steep trails. I can draw. I can hug people I love.) Try to build it to 100.
3. Type or print Psalm 139:14 on a sticky note or index card and put it on your mirror. Read it over before you leave your house.
4. Remember a time when you weren't consumed with disliking your body. Think about how you felt then and purpose to have those same feelings now.
5. Do a physical activity that is gentle to your body. Don't do it to lose weight, but to feel good and be stronger.
6. Make arrangements to sleep in as late as you can one day. When you awake, thank God for the rest your body received, then stretch out and enjoy the pleasure of that rest.
7. Get a massage.
8. As you lie down at night, thank God for all the activities you could do or participate in because you have a body.
9. Wrestle with a child or play with your dog. Get down on the floor and enjoy a good playtime.
10. Take a walk and thank God for your body as you walk.

As you begin practicing these exercises regularly, you will find a new energy to heal. The energy comes from the time you are able to put into thinking positively about your body and from interrupting the ways you are stuck in putting down your body. Body hate breeds more body hate.

How Do We Stop the Perfection Cycle?

Do you better understand why the solution to body-image problems is spiritual? Do you see that what you are up against isn't just modern media and culture? A war is raging for your soul. If you are a Christian, Satan lost you to Christ when you accepted Him as your Savior, but he still wants to keep you in bondage from the freedom of knowing how loved you really are. Prayer is a powerful tool in overcoming the trap of negative body image. Pray this prayer as you end this chapter.

Dear heavenly Father and Creator of my body:

I recognize that I struggle to know and live out what is truly perfect. I can see how my heart is drawn to Satan's message that perfection is the answer. I can easily get focused on wanting perfect beauty rather than wanting You.

In the strong name of Jesus Christ, I stand against the world of advertising, diet, the beauty industry, my vanity, and Satan himself. I resist every force that would seek to distract me from who I really am and what You desire for me to do in and through this body You gave me. I reject the distorted concepts and ideas that make body perfection sound plausible and desirable. I oppose every attempt to keep me from knowing full fellowship with You. I commit to completing this study with an open heart to be transformed into true perfection through Jesus Christ. Amen.

Please know that I am praying this prayer for you too.

Discussion Questions

1. What do you consider perfect beauty?

2. Why do you think God created us with so many variations in appearance?

3. Go over each of the 10 statements on the Perfection Scale on pages 30–31 and discuss why they are perfectionist assumptions and not facts.

4. Why could Satan be called "the father of beauty perfectionism"?

5. At what times or in what situations do you struggle with your body image the most?

6. Share prayer requests about how you are finding victory or defeat over body image, as well as other issues for which you need prayer. Repeat the prayer on page 45 in unison as you close your meeting.

CHAPTER THREE

The Truth About Beauty

*M*isty got pregnant the first time she had sex—the night of her senior prom. Throughout the summer that followed, she lived in denial that she could possibly be pregnant. Before she went to college, at her annual physical, she was finally forced to face the truth. Her church and parents were overwhelmingly supportive. Surrounded by God's grace, Misty made a difficult but loving decision to allow her baby daughter to be adopted by a Christian couple. There was joy and heartache for all involved.

Her stretch marks were a repulsive reminder of the high cost of sin, and they threatened to send Misty into despair. When she looked at them, she condemned herself for being so stupid and getting pregnant and managing to make such a mess of her life.

What kind of good Christian man could ever love a woman who has done what I've done and who looks like this? is the question that ran through her head. It took a lot of faith to confront the disparaging remarks that erupted throughout her day. Misty needed to be built up by believing God's Word and becoming anchored in His love for her.

Misty's hopes for human love and romance aren't over because she has a few stretch marks. In fact, they may help steer her to the right man after all. The kind of man she needs is the kind of man who will love her unconditionally, the way God does. She can find that hope as she believes what God says about her and her body in His Word.

What God Says About Our Bodies

What does God say about our bodies? He says a lot. His wisdom is in direct contrast to the wisdom of our culture. As you read this brief survey of what God says about bodies, be sensitive to any scripture you sense God is speaking particularly to you. If a word or phrase in one of the verses stands out to you, write it down in your journal. Even if you don't understand fully what that word means at the time, it may become more apparent later. When God speaks to us through His Word, healing takes place in our souls.

God Is Not Ashamed of Your Body

God isn't ashamed of the bodies He created for us. He doesn't judge us by what our bodies look like either. Nowhere in God's Word is anyone put down for his or her body. You never find God putting one of His prophets on a diet, unless it is a spiritual discipline such as fasting, abstaining from certain foods, and so on. God doesn't hold beauty contests or make comparisons. To Him, every body is beautiful. No exceptions!

Let's look at Genesis 1:26–27, 31 to understand how God feels about our bodies. You will see that it is the opposite of shame.

Then God said, "Let us make man in our image, in our like-
ness, and let them rule over the fish of the sea and the birds of
the air, over the livestock, over all the earth, and over all the
creatures that move along the ground." So God created man in
his own image, in the image of God he created him; male and
female he created them. . . . God saw all that he had made,
and it was very good. And there was evening, and there was
morning—the sixth day.

🌱 In whose image were you created?

🌱 What did God say after He created man and woman?

Human beings are the only part of God's creation that contain the
image of God. He views us as His image bearers, even with stretch
marks. He feels the complete opposite of shame about our bodies. To
Him, the way we are created is very good. Everything God made is
good. He doesn't want to melt anyone down and start over. He is very
pleased with the final touch of His creation we call the universe.

🌱 Imagine that God has just created you in the garden. Look
at your body right now. Don't look in a mirror; just look
at the parts of your body that you can see with your own
eyes.

🌱 Find 10 parts of your body that you can praise God for as the
master Creator of your body. Look at your toes and watch
them wiggle. Praise God for making your toes wiggle. Rub
your hands together and feel the smoothness and warmth.
Thank God that you can feel comfort through a touch.

🎍 Thinking of God as the Creator of our bodies, how do you think He feels when we hate and abuse the flesh that He made? How would you feel if you were the creator?

I'm embarrassed by the places I have hair.

God Knows What Your Body Needs

"Therefore I tell you, do not worry about your life, what you will eat or drink; or about your body, what you will wear. Is not life more important than food, and the body more important than clothes? Look at the birds of the air; they do not sow or reap or store away in barns, and yet your heavenly Father feeds them. Are you not much more valuable than they? Who of you by worrying can add a single hour to his life?

"And why do you worry about clothes? See how the lilies of the field grow. They do not labor or spin. Yet I tell you that not even Solomon in all his splendor was dressed like one of these. If that is how God clothes the grass of the field, which is here today and tomorrow is thrown into the fire, will he not much more clothe you, O you of little faith? So do not worry, saying, 'What shall we eat?' or 'What shall we drink?' or 'What shall we wear?' For the pagans run after all these things, and your heavenly Father knows that you need them. But seek first his kingdom and his righteousness, and all these things will be given to you as well." (Matthew 6:25–33)

🎍 Why do you think God wants us to seek Him as a way to provide for our bodies?

Your life is more than what you put on, put in, or experience with
your body. It is natural for people to worry about issues that concern
their bodies. God is trying to tell us that if we learn to trust Him with
our natural bodily concerns, He will provide for them. He is the One
who gives us the air we breathe and the food we eat. God knows what
our bodies need. He wants us to trust Him to provide for our naked-
ness, our hunger, and even the number of days we will live on this
earth.

We rarely give God credit for meeting our daily needs. Have you
thanked God for the food you've eaten today? Have you recognized
God's provision in the clothes on your back right now? When was the
last time you thanked God for giving you oxygen to breathe?

*I had open-heart surgery and my chest
and stomach look like a tic-tac-toe board
from the unsightly scars.*

In my own life I recognize that God has provided clothes for me,
and even certain dresses in answer to specific prayers. I remember a
Christmas season that was extra tight financially. I was to attend a
Christmas party but didn't like the clothes I had to wear. While I was out
Christmas shopping, I prayed that God would help me find a dress for
the party for under $30. I found a dress I liked on the sale rack for
$29.99. I was so grateful for it as I went up to the counter to pay. When
the sales clerk rang it up at the register, the total came to $11.99. There
was an extra discount on sale items that day. God showed me that
indeed He does do more than I could ever ask or think (Ephesians 3:20).

The amount of time we spend worrying about what we will wear reveals the level of our trust in God. When we seek God first, we discover how "all these things" are taken care of by Him. We either learn that we don't need certain items after all, or we see God blessing us far beyond our understanding.

Your Soul Is More Valuable Than Your Body

"Do not be afraid of those who kill the body but cannot kill the soul. Rather, be afraid of the One who can destroy both soul and body in hell. Are not two sparrows sold for a penny? Yet not one of them will fall to the ground apart from the will of your Father. And even the very hairs of your head are all numbered. So don't be afraid; you are worth more than many sparrows." (Matthew 10:28–31)

🌱 Who or what murders your soul?

🌱 Why should you be as afraid of him as you are of murderers?

It is natural to fear those who can kill our bodies. We are afraid of attack dogs, rapists, murderers, and drunk drivers. Each of these can kill us or inflict great harm on our bodies. Our natural response is fear. But do we fear the murder that may be taking place in our souls? Do we assess the damage that body hate does to who we are and how we see ourselves? God encourages us to have the same kind of fear of soul murderers as we do of body murderers.

My soul has been damaged by materialism, anger, bitterness, busyness, covetousness, and more. The frightening reality about soul murder is that it is a silent killer. Many times the victim doesn't even recognize that her soul is dead.

I still remember the day I noticed a deadness in my soul. I was a young mom, and my husband was at the top of his field at a very young age. All I thought about was the house I could buy, the car I could drive, and the clothes I could wear. I was a regular attendee of church, but an infrequent worshiper of God. My soul was dead. Then God gave me the job of chairing an AIDS committee, a potentially divisive and disruptive issue in the church in the 1980s.

Even though my soul was dead, I recognized that the most important thing our committee needed to do was pray. We were fervent in prayer for our church members as they responded to the information that we brought before them. We prayed for wisdom as we prepared our church nurseries and children's areas for the children and adults inflicted with that terrible disease that has brought so much pain, hurt, and misunderstanding. God blessed in every way, and His will was accomplished in that church. That in itself was wonderful.

During that experience, my soul came back to life. My soul was revived by the faith required to successfully lead that committee and our church to a compassionate and wise response to individuals inflicted with AIDS. I hadn't realized that my soul was dead, and evidently others hadn't either, or I would never have been asked to chair that committee.

Waking up from spiritual deadness is a powerful experience. When you aren't aware that you are spiritually dead, you don't feel a thing. You go about your life in the same way you always have. When you come in out of the cold and start feeling the warmth of God's presence again, it begins to hurt a little. I was humbled and scared; I knew I was in way over my head. I was embarrassed that my faith had shriveled and was so far from where it had been when I was a teenager. It hurt to face the truth. Amazingly, I came alive again. Once the thawing out was complete, I could sense the Spirit's leading in my life. Is your soul alive today?

God Wants You to Offer Your Body to Him

In the same way, count yourselves dead to sin but alive to God in Christ Jesus. Therefore do not let sin reign in your mortal body so that you obey its evil desires. Do not offer the parts of your body to sin, as instruments of wickedness, but rather offer yourselves to God, as those who have been brought from death to life; and offer the parts of your body to him as instruments of righteousness. For sin shall not be your master, because you are not under law, but under grace. (Romans 6:11–14)

❦ How do you allow sin to reign in your body?

❦ How can you offer your body as an instrument of righteousness?

You have a choice to make about your body. Without being conscious of this choice, your sin nature will lead you to offer your body to sin. Oh, it may not be hideous sin—not murder, theft, or adultery. But you might just give your mind to television, which interferes with your decision to follow God. Out of boredom or anger you may offer your body to food binges, or allow your tongue to spread gossip, cruelly criticizing or harming others. There are endless ways to allow sin to reign in your body.

In place of offering your body to sin, God instructs you to offer your body as an instrument of righteousness. I believe I offer my body as an instrument of righteousness in my church as I lead and participate in prayer. When I dress modestly, my body is an instrument of righteousness. When I use my hands to feed the poor, my body becomes an instrument of righteousness.

See your body as a gift you can give to God. He does not claim you or your body, even though He made you and provides for your very existence. God invites you to dedicate yourself and your body to Him and His will. If you don't give your body to God, it will naturally serve evil. You make this choice every day.

Everyone always tells me that I have such a pretty
face—meaning I could be really pretty if I lost weight.

God Tells You to Protect Yourself from Sexual Sin

It is God's will that you should be sanctified: that you should avoid sexual immorality; that each of you should learn to control his own body in a way that is holy and honorable, not in passionate lust like the heathen, who do not know God; and that in this matter no one should wrong his brother or take advantage of him. The Lord will punish men for all such sins, as we have already told you and warned you. For God did not call us to be impure, but to live a holy life. Therefore, he who rejects this instruction does not reject man but God, who gives you his Holy Spirit. (1 Thessalonians 4:3–8)

❦ What instructions does God give about our sexuality in this passage?

I read these passages as a teenager and now believe that they give the clearest direction for dealing with sexual standards in dating relationships. Singles are taught that they are not to have sex before marriage, but what about the in-between? How far can you go?

According to this passage, you shouldn't be involved in any sexual activity before marriage that would make you feel that you are losing control. Even more important than that, you shouldn't be involved in any sexual activity that would cause your partner to lose control. This led me to decide that my sexual standards would be to only hug, hold hands, and kiss before marriage. A standard like that is certainly going against what the world says is okay.

> *When I was a child, my shirt caught on fire*
> *and I have unsightly scars on my back. I avoid*
> *clothes and events where my scars might show.*
> *I even try to hide them from my husband.*

Decisions we make to follow God's standards allow Him to sanctify our bodies. Being sanctified in your body means setting your body apart from the world for God's purposes. I want to encourage you that it is never too late to yield your body to God. Even if you have already been sexually immoral, He promises to forgive you and cleanse you if you confess your sin to Him (1 John 1:9). You can be cleansed from your sexual past and allow God to sanctify you for your sexual future.

God Will Reward You for How You Live in Your Body

Therefore we are always confident and know that as long as we are at home in the body we are away from the Lord. We live by faith, not by sight. We are confident, I say, and would prefer to be away from the body and at home with the Lord. So we make it our goal to please him, whether we are at home in the body or away from it. For we must all appear before the judgment seat of Christ, that each one may receive what is due him for the things done while in the body, whether good or bad. (2 Corinthians 5:6–10)

♈ When we appear before the judgment seat, what will we be held accountable for?

When Christians stand before the judgment seat of Christ described in 2 Corinthians 5:10, we will be judged for what we did while in our bodies. These bodies of ours are like a marker of time. They are in themselves a countdown revealing how much time we have left to serve God on earth. Of course, this isn't the case for all believers. Some healthy children and adults are called home to heaven without any warning from their bodies. The judgment you will receive will be about a specific amount of time—the exact amount of time that you existed in your body.

God Wants You to Glorify Him with Your Body

I eagerly expect and hope that I will in no way be ashamed, but will have sufficient courage so that now as always Christ will be exalted in my body, whether by life or by death. (Philippians 1:20)

His 90th birthday occurred on a Sunday. While his wife and some relatives were home that morning preparing for his birthday celebration, Mr. Cantrell made a special request of the pastor. Mr. Cantrell had been the president of the Baptist foundation for 22 years. He had faithfully served in his church as a deacon and men's Sunday school teacher, and was even made a deacon for life. On the Sunday of his 90th birthday, he came forward to rededicate whatever years he had left on this earth to serve God. There wasn't a dry eye in the house. What a beautiful way to live in the body.

♈ Who do you know who has truly exalted Christ with his or her body whether by life or by death?

Your Body Will Be Transformed in Heaven

Who, by the power that enables him to bring everything under his control, will transform our lowly bodies so that they will be like his glorious body. (Philippians 3:21)

➤ What do you think our bodies will be like when they are glorified as Christ's was?

We don't know the answer to this question for sure, but there are clues in Scripture that give us some ideas about our eternal bodies. Jesus moved freely through walls after He rose from the dead (John 20:19).

The "Beam me up, Scottie" mode of transportation seen in *Star Trek* isn't just science fiction. Philip experienced it after he witnessed to the Ethiopian eunuch (Acts 8:39). He was suddenly taken up from the river and appeared in Azotus. Jesus also disappeared (Luke 24:31) and was taken up into heaven (Mark 16:19).

Jesus' voice could be recognized (John 20:16), although many times He appeared and wasn't instantly recognized by His voice or outward appearance, but rather by His actions (Luke 24:13–32). We will not have the same desire to marry as we do now (Matthew 22:30). I don't think we will be worried about cellulite or fat cells. Our eternal bodies will be fantastic and freeing at the same time.

God Wants You to Be Concerned About Others' Bodily Needs

Suppose a brother or sister is without clothes and daily food. If one of you says to him, "Go, I wish you well; keep warm and well fed," but does nothing about his physical needs, what good is it? In the same way, faith by itself, if it is not accompanied by action, is dead. (James 2:15–17)

🌱 Should Christians be concerned about the physical needs
of others?

It is always convicting to read Scripture passages like this one in
light of the enormous physical needs that exist in our world today. I do
my little bit, but I know of many more needs than I meet. Sometimes
I think, *If we spent only half the time and money we spend on our beauty
regimens on the poor, how many needs would be left?* Once a month I
send about $30 to Compassion International to support a needy child.
I think of it as my manicure money, even though I would spend more
than that if I got regular manicures every other week. Do your beauty
needs consume you to the point that you are not even aware of the genu-
ine bodily needs of others?

God Knows Humans Overemphasize Looks
in Evaluating Character

When Samuel was instructed to look for a new king among Jesse's sons,
God told him: "Do not consider his appearance or his height, for I
have rejected him. The LORD does not look at the things man looks at.
Man looks at the outward appearance, but the LORD looks at the heart"
(1 Samuel 16:7).

Samuel was a great prophet of God. His very conception was
established in prayer. His mother, Hannah, was barren and went to the
temple to pray for a child. (See 1 Samuel 1 for the story.) His entire life
was dedicated to God, and he remained faithful to Him throughout his
life, in spite of the poor examples of leadership provided by the priest
Eli and his sons, under whom he served.

Samuel knew the Word of God and obeyed it painstakingly. When
God determined that Saul should no longer be the king of Israel and

decided to have Samuel anoint a new king, He gave the warning you just read. He told Samuel not to be surprised if the king God chose didn't look like much of a king.

If a great prophet of God like Samuel can be misled by appearances, no wonder the same thing happens to you and me. We need to heed the same warning about appearances that God gave Samuel. We need to be more concerned about how beautiful our hearts are than concerned about our looks.

God Does Not Place the Emphasis on Outward Appearance that Humans Do

Let's consider Jesus' appearance: "He grew up before him like a tender shoot, and like a root out of dry ground. He had no beauty or majesty to attract us to him, nothing in his appearance that we should desire him" (Isaiah 53:2).

🌱 How would you design your body if you were creating one for yourself?

If you or I could decide how we were to look, we would probably throw in a lot of extra-beautiful characteristics. God purposefully chose to leave them out of Jesus' human body when He became man. God will not be holding beauty pageants in heaven. He created the differences in physical characteristics that in combination create true beauty. God certainly enjoys beauty, but one person's beauty does not diminish someone else's in God's view.

Misty wouldn't have thought stretch marks could be beauty marks. But Linda, her baby's adoptive mother, would have gladly endured 10 times as many stretch marks just to be a mother. Misty began to realize that those stretch marks are beauty marks to God. She did a beautiful and loving thing by not aborting her daughter and by allowing her to be raised by loving parents.

God Knows Women Are Particularly Interested in Looking Nice
Let's look at 1 Peter 3:3–4: "Your beauty should not come from outward adornment, such as braided hair and the wearing of gold jewelry and fine clothes. Instead, it should be that of your inner self, the unfading beauty of a gentle and quiet spirit, which is of great worth in God's sight."

  ❦ What kind of adorning does God think is beautiful in
    women?

Women are adorners. Something inside most of us drives us to look our best. God doesn't condemn that. He does condemn getting overly caught up in outward beauty, though. He knows that is important to us, but He wants so much more for us. God encourages women not to ignore true beauty by merely focusing on externals. He longs for us to cultivate the internal qualities of a gentle and quiet spirit.

To develop our internal qualities, it's important to spend time with God. We need to rely on the Holy Spirit to fill us with love, joy, peace, patience, kindness, goodness, faithfulness, gentleness, and self-control (Galatians 5:22–23). A gentle and quiet spirit is the result of placing your full trust in God—not in your looks, talents, or abilities.

God Is Not Opposed to Nice Clothes and Good Grooming
Consider the Proverbs 31 woman: "She makes coverings for her bed; she is clothed in fine linen and purple" (Proverbs 31:22).

❦ Is it okay for Christian women to wear fine clothing?

This outstanding woman's clothing was of a fine quality, but her clothes are mentioned only briefly among her many wonderful characteristics—caring for the needs of the household, working with her hands, helping the poor, and other activities.

The list of this woman's qualities has challenged women through the centuries. There appears to be simply nothing that she couldn't do. Some say that it was all the servants in her household that helped her get so much done. In any case, she was a very dutiful, productive woman. It is liberating in a way to think that her clothes of fine linen were mentioned.

It is not bad or sinful for women to like attractive clothes. God does not forbid you to decorate your home in beauty and comfort. It is only when you let pursuing beauty get out of hand that it becomes a problem. It is natural to want to look the best you can, but you can look as nice when you buy your clothes at a discount store as you do when you buy them at the finest clothing store around. The important thing isn't the label—it's the balance you create in your life.

You Can Be Outwardly Beautiful and Still Be Unattractive

Proverbs has much to say on this subject:

> Like a gold ring in a pig's snout is a beautiful woman who shows no discretion. (Proverbs 11:22)

> Charm is deceptive, and beauty is fleeting; but a woman who fears the LORD is to be praised. (Proverbs 31:30)

❦ How is it possible to be outwardly beautiful, but not attractive?

❦ What is necessary to be attractive?

It's not just how you look on the outside that makes you beautiful. Beauty is a combination of many characteristics. First Corinthians 13, the great love chapter, is a wonderful description of what God would consider truly beautiful. Let it remind you of someone in your life whose beauty is defined not by her physical characteristics but by her actions.

Our Bodies Are God's Dwelling Place on Earth

Do you not know that your body is a temple of the Holy Spirit, who is in you, whom you have received from God? You are not your own; you were bought at a price. Therefore honor God with your body. (1 Corinthians 6:19–20)

❦ What does it mean to you that your body is the temple of God? (If you are a Christian, the Holy Spirit lives inside of you.)

❦ How can you honor God with your body?

It just blows me away to think that my body is the place that the God of the universe chooses to dwell. I want to treat my body like God's temple. I want to keep it pure from sexual immorality. I want to use it to glorify God. His presence validates the honor He places on your body. God himself is eager to dwell in your body. He has made your body His temple on earth.

God Made Our Bodies to Bring Reverence and Praise to Him

"I praise you because I am fearfully and wonderfully made; your works are wonderful, I know that full well" (Psalm 139:14).

The number one reason to honor the body God gave you is because He made you. King David, the author of Psalm 139, understood this in a unique way.

Occasionally I catch the *Oprah Winfrey Show* while I'm cooking dinner. Over the years I have been amazed by her poor body image. She is constantly putting herself down for not being skinny. So I was thrilled for her the day the program about a new medical test aired. It was about an X-ray machine used to detect medical problems before symptoms occur. The machine scans the body from several different perspectives.

After having the test and viewing the inside of her body, Oprah experienced a dramatic shift. She said, "I've changed my whole paradigm, because you know I've been on every diet in America. Some I invented, some I borrowed from other people, but for the first time after doing this test, I decided I'm no longer going to eat or exercise for my hips. I'm doing it for my heart."[1] During the program she mentioned several times that she loved her heart, and that she hadn't eaten a potato chip since she saw the scan of her heart. Oprah had a King David experience. She got a better glimpse into her body and the mystery it is.

God Loves You Just the Way You Are

Not liking your body is a symptom of not knowing who you are to God. First John 4:18 says, "There is no fear in love." Your fear of being

unacceptable is evidence that you are not fully embracing God's acceptance of you. Being immersed in God's love is the remedy for discour-
agement about how you look. When you become energized by His
love and acceptance, you'll find balance in your efforts to care for your
body. You'll no longer eat and exercise out of fear and shame, but out
of a desire to care for your body.

🌱 Write a letter to yourself from God expressing His love for
   you and how He wants you to think about your body.

If God did write you such a letter expressing His love for you and
your body, this is what I think He might say:

Dear _____ (your name):
   I want you to know the joy of believing you are wonderfully made (Psalm 139:14). Indeed, you are made just right!
Satan is trying to deceive you into thinking your
_____ (body flaw) is evidence that I don't love you,
but that is another one of his lies. I love you completely! I know
everything about you and nothing stops me from loving you
(Romans 8:38–39). I understand that you wish you didn't have
_____ (body flaw). But you will miss out on what is
important on earth if you don't receive your limitations and
body flaws as part of my plan for you (Psalm 139:15–17).
   Bring all your worries to me, and I will replace them with
peace (Matthew 11:28–30). I have great and wonderful opportunities for you to share my love with others in your world who
don't know how much I love them, too. Receive my truth that
you are beautiful, and let me show you the beautiful life I want
you to have.

🌱 What else would God say? What has He been saying to you through this study? Get started on your letter and share it with a friend.

> *My most humiliating experience of being overweight was the day I got kicked off the amusement park ride because I couldn't buckle the seat belt. I left my family to enjoy the ride and walked the plank into deeper shame and contempt for who I am.*

Victory Is Possible

Working on your body image depends on changing the way you think more than on changing your body. Working on your body image will result in changes in your body, mind, and soul. God created you with a mysterious connection between the three. As you change your thinking, your body benefits by discovering more energy. Your soul is tended as you discover God's truth about yourself. It's a huge spiritual breakthrough.

You see, when you are thinking about truth (God's Word), taking care of your body through proper rest, eating, and exercise, and tending to your spiritual self, then all three parts of you—body, mind, and soul—function in balance. When you stop making your body the scapegoat for all the pain and hurt you have suffered, equilibrium and balance will enter your life.

🌱 Remember that chronological survey you completed in chapter one? Are you ready to tear it out of your journal and throw those memories and experiences away? If so, do that as a sign of the victory God has given you.

It's time to make practical changes in your mind, will, and emotions. It's time to break the chains of body hate. Misty's stretch marks have faded a bit, and the evidence of being anchored in God's Word is more apparent in her life. Presently, she is dating a seminary student who treats her the way God wants her to be treated. Because she has focused on God's Word as truth, she no longer sees her stretch marks as an obstacle to love, but as a symbol of her love.

The most beautiful, perfect Creator of the universe longs to dwell in your body. He wants to live in you. He chooses your body with all its flaws!

Discussion Questions

1. How does your body reflect God's image?

2. Share ways God meets your bodily needs.

3. How can you glorify God with your body?

4. What are some ways you can meet/are meeting the physical needs of others?

5. How can you fight your human tendency to look on the outside rather than at the heart?

6. How does God's Word help you get the right perspective on your body?

CHAPTER FOUR

A Beautiful Mind

Laurie's double mastectomy with reconstructive surgery took place without major complications. Recovery was difficult and included chemotherapy, but two years after her last chemo treatment she was glad to be alive. She'd just received good news from her doctor, and her life had taken on a sense of normalcy again. Laurie hadn't been focusing on her disfigured body as much as she had been concerned with just staying alive. The good news that her cancer was in remission allowed her to stop and consider the body she was left with in the aftermath of cancer.

Did she love and accept this body? In one sense she felt betrayed by it. In another sense she was just like everyone else, feeling ashamed of her scars, unnatural shape, an extra layer of fat, and varicose veins. Her hair had grown back in a texture and color she hardly recognized. In the scope of two years her normal body flaws had transformed into massive alterations (in her opinion). But after what she had been through, she would never consider optional surgery to correct any of these body flaws. So what was she supposed to do now?

Accepting Your Body Starts with What You Believe

Laurie needed to start by confronting what she believed about herself. A healthy body image starts in transforming the mind. What you think about your body is your body image. If you think negatively about your body, then you have a negative body image. If you think positively about your body, you have a healthy body image. A healthy body image has no correlation to what you weigh or how you look.

> *I feel pressure to look as good as all the other doctors' wives. I don't have time to know if I really like how I look, I'm so busy trying to look better.*

You do not have direct control over your feelings, but you do have control over what you think and how you behave. God's Word challenges you to be transformed in your mind.

Mind Makeover

Research has pinpointed the specific part of the brain that controls your sense of self.[1] The study shows how front temporal dementia causes individuals to change their political or religious beliefs, the type of clothes they wear, foods they like, and more. This research confirms the importance of making over your mind and the power of your thoughts over the rest of your life.

In Matthew 16, Jesus rebuked Peter for not having the right mindset. After Jesus predicted His upcoming death, Peter responded, "This shall never happen to you!"

"Jesus turned and said to Peter, 'Get behind me, Satan! You are a stumbling block to me; you do not have in mind the things of God, but the things of men'" (Matthew 16:22–23).

It is very important to survey the thoughts that guide your life. Do you have in mind the things of God, or the things of men? What you focus on will make a big difference in how you live and enjoy your life. You may be surprised to find how much your mind is influenced by the world when it comes to beauty.

My reason for including so much of God's Word in this book is so your mind will be penetrated by the truth that sets you free. At times in my life, I've had the mind of the world toward my body, and at other times the mind of God. I can promise you that having the mind of God is so much better! It's the way I have learned to be comfortable in my own skin.

> Therefore, I urge you, brothers, in view of God's mercy, to
> offer your bodies as living sacrifices, holy and pleasing to
> God—this is your spiritual act of worship. Do not conform
> any longer to the pattern of this world, but be transformed by
> the renewing of your mind. Then you will be able to test and
> approve what God's will is—his good, pleasing and perfect
> will. (Romans 12:1–2)

🌷 What are you not supposed to do according to this passage? What are you asked to do?

If your desire is to accept and use your body the way God's Word instructs, it is clear from this passage that you will be going against the tide of the world. God gave you your body. He invites you to offer it back to Him as a living sacrifice. He is not interested in human sacrifices as the pagan gods are—literally giving your body to be burned or consumed. Rather, God asks you to live in your body (living), yet to live in your body for His glory, not your own (sacrifice). If you have been moved by God's marvelous mercy toward you, you can respond in love by giving your life (which includes your body) to Him.

How can you be a living sacrifice? You allow God to work in you, and you believe the things that He says are the truth, rather than what the world says. You replace your old belief system, which is based on the world's philosophies, with God's Word. As my good friend and speaker Ron Rand says, "You've got to get the *L* out!" When he says this, those in the audience do a double take to make sure they heard him right. It makes the point well, though. You need to get the *L* out and stop worrying what the *world* says; rather, center your life on what the *Word* says.

If you listen to the world, you are valued only if you wear the latest style of clothing on a perfect body. If you listen to the Word, you are valued when you wear appropriate clothes that fit your budget on a body that contains a heart that loves and lives for God.

Let's look at what the world tells us versus what the truth is about common body-image myths.

Seven Lies the World Tells About Our Bodies

*Lie One: If I change something about my body,
I will finally like myself.*
Get up early on a weekend morning and start clicking through the cable television channels, and you will see how pervasive this message is. Whatever bothers you about your appearance, a product exists to fix it for five easy installments of $49.99.

These television infomercials provide testimonials of women and men whose lives have been changed by "amazing" products. Though the products may vary, the story is always the same: These people went from suffering low self-esteem to feeling on top of the world after they used these products to diet, enlarge breasts, replace hair, remove unwanted hair, clear up acne, erase wrinkles, trim waists, firm thighs, and so on.

Think about this. If you could purchase a product that would change the part of your body that you dislike most, would it raise your self-esteem? I acknowledge that people do feel a little better about themselves after they receive positive feedback about something they have changed, such as losing weight. But the positive feelings usually don't last long, and people often start to fixate on some other flaw.

Your self-esteem isn't as much about how you look right now as it is about what you think about how you look right now. Consider the following illustration from Jane's life.

Jane went on a fad diet and quickly lost 50 pounds. After the first 25 were gone, people started to notice and say positive things to Jane. By the time she lost all 50 (in four months), several of her friends noticed and wanted to know what she was doing. It felt awesome to know she was an example for others.

I was born with a cleft lip, and although surgery has fixed it, I still feel a little like a freak.

Tim, a man Jane had worked with for a long time and greatly admired, asked her for a date after she had lost 50 pounds. She couldn't have been happier. She knew that he would never have asked her when she was heavier, and she didn't mind. She believed that she was worthy of him now that she was skinny. It seemed as if Jane's self-esteem had totally changed.

The night of the date, Tim called and canceled. He said he was sick. Jane didn't believe him. She knew that he had seen her in the break room eating a small piece of chocolate birthday cake. She believed that he canceled the date because he began to doubt that getting involved with her was a wise thing. She assumed that he thought she would gain back all the weight and she couldn't stay thin.

Even though Jane had lost the 50 pounds and eating the piece of cake didn't affect her weight at all, she returned to being the same self-loathing person she had been before her diet. The increase in self-esteem was shallow and temporary. Nothing of substance had changed in the way Jane saw herself.

Jane found out later that Tim really had been sick. He was out of work the whole next week with the flu. Jane realized through this experience that changing her body was not enough to change her self-esteem problems. She still felt just as bad about herself, if not worse.

The truth: Healthy self-esteem comes from believing in the value God places in you, not in the value man assigns to you.

 Check yourself:
  Do you believe that even if you changed _____ (whatever you dislike most about your body), you could still dislike yourself?

Lie Two: My outward appearance is the most
important thing about me.
It is part of human development for adolescents to become overly preoccupied with their physical appearance, but some women never move beyond this developmental stage. You recognize it in their wardrobes. The overabundance of clothes shows the emphasis they put on appearances. Their checkbooks reveal their insecurities about their looks.

In chapter two you tallied the amount of time you spend on your looks. Was it a reasonable amount of time? Could you spend less time on your appearance? Are you unable to make a change because you believe this statement to be true: "How I look is the most important thing about me"?

Here's an assignment for you: Go to the grocery store or some other public place without makeup on and without your hair done. Another recommendation is to fast from buying new clothes, makeup, or other beauty products for three months. (Don't go on a shopping spree before you do this, either.) Wear last year's bathing suit. Use up some of the beauty products that are cluttering your bathroom drawers and cabinets.

Surviving breast cancer helped Laurie realize that her health is more important than her appearance. She may not like everything about the way her body was changed by surgery and chemo, but she's glad she has more days left on the earth, and she wants to live them free of despair about her body.

The truth: Your outward appearance is what people will first judge you by, but your personality, self-confidence, talents and abilities, and spiritual sensitivity are each vital to who you are as well.

✿ Check yourself:
Do you think it is wrong for people to accept or reject you on the basis of your appearance alone?

Lie Three: I can look like a movie star or fashion model if I diet enough, do the right exercises, and use the right products.
Jeanine had been bulimic since her twenties. It started in college when she threw up regularly in order to have a flat stomach for spring break. It turned into a 13-year habit that consumed her life.

She can still recall how she felt about her body back then. Basically, she felt attractive and healthy. The only thing she didn't like was the little ring of fat that encircled her abdomen. Then she read a magazine article about a top fashion model that included pictures of the model working out and wearing a bikini revealing a totally flat stomach. The article convinced Jeanine that if she followed this model's diet and exercise plan, she could have a perfectly flat stomach too.

With spring break just around the corner, she forced herself to vomit more frequently to achieve movie-star results. After she threw up, Jeanine was convinced that her stomach was flatter. So she kept on and on and hasn't stopped since, although she has often tried.

People develop eating disorders for many reasons. In Jeanine's case, although there were other contributing factors, there's no doubt that she honestly believed she could make her stomach look like the model's and that she ought to do so.

When Jeanine and I talked, I asked her to bring in pictures of her relatives. She had been to a family reunion on her mother's side recently, so we looked over a group picture of aunts and uncles, cousins, and siblings. About half of those in the picture had similar body types. None were tall and lanky (like the model). Most of the women were between five feet three inches and five feet six inches. They were average in weight. All of the women had a little more plumpness around their stomach area. Jeanine knew for a fact that most of them didn't eat right or exercise.

But her Aunt Jenny, who was 65 at the time the picture was taken, had been a gym teacher and was a picture of health all her life. When we zeroed in on Aunt Jenny, whom Jeanine never considered fat, she could see the little bit of plumpness in her stomach area too. This helped Jeanine face the fact that she could not have the flat stomach of the famous model, even after 13 years of throwing up. But bulimia had given her a mixed-up metabolism and rotting teeth. At 33, her stomach was rounder than it had ever been and she was in terrible health.

It will be helpful for you to take a good long look at the genetic makeup you inherited. Look at your blood relatives and observe any dominant body characteristics that you have in common. Those of us who are 40 and older can develop a realistic expectation of healthy bodies by considering pictures of relatives rather than movie stars.

The generations before ours seldom tortured and mistreated their bodies on a quest for thinness. For the younger generation, though, this exercise may prove more difficult. Some of your relatives may have distorted their body shape through eating disorders, surgery, and chronic dieting. On the other hand, you may have relatives who have abused their bodies through obesity. This doesn't mean that you should just give in and do the same. You can recognize the genetic predisposition you may have toward obesity and work toward keeping your body healthy in spite of it.

Here's a helpful exercise for you: Get out photo albums and look at pictures of your blood relatives. Record your answers to the following questions in your journal:

🌾 How is your body shape similar to that of your relatives?

🌾 How is your body different from that of your relatives? What is most natural for you to look like if you consider the characteristics you see in these family pictures and in yourself?

🌾 What is the best look for your body if you take good care of it?

The truth: We will tend to look more like our blood relatives than movie stars and models.

🌱 Do you believe that you can't and you shouldn't have to look like a movie star or model?

Lie Four: Attractive people don't have any problems.
The only thing Stella wanted in life was to be attractive. She'd felt ugly and inferior in high school. During college and into her first job, she lost weight and learned how to style her hair and wear makeup in an attractive way. People who knew her in high school were amazed at their five-year reunion. She had been transformed.

The main reason Stella wanted to look good was so she wouldn't have to feel the pain of loneliness anymore. In high school she thought the lives of the pretty and popular cheerleaders were perfect. She envied them. But looking like a cheerleader wasn't the answer to her problems. In fact, the closer Stella got to being accepted by the type of girls she'd always envied, the more she realized that their problems were just as bad as, if not worse than, her own.

The truth is that we all have problems. Some of our problems can be made worse because of appearance. Often, more is expected of attractive people. It is true, on the other hand, that less attractive people have been discriminated against. If you think improving your appearance will make all your troubles go away, you are kidding yourself. You may be less troubled by your appearance, but you still must face the same amount of pressure and difficulty that you did before.

The truth: We all have troubles in this life. Being attractive doesn't make anyone immune to problems.

❦ Check yourself:
Do you believe that even if you changed your body flaws
the way you wanted to, you would still feel pain and have
troubles?

Lie Five: Being overweight is a sin.
Remember Christine from earlier chapters? She is the one who,
although overweight, was honored to be asked to take part in the
church fashion show. Her response was a direct contrast to Marybeth's,
who looked more the model type than Christine did. Marybeth imme-
diately refused because she hated her body so much.

Christine didn't come to that place of peace about her body easily.
She got there only through the love and support she found in her relationship with God. One area that had blocked her closeness to God
was her disgust with her weight. She believed she was a bad Christian
because she couldn't keep her weight under control. Christine pro-
jected her mom's feelings about her weight onto God. She automatically thought He hated her being fat, even though He accepted her as
His child. She didn't try to get close to God because she felt she was an
embarrassment to Him.

I can't even find my waist anymore.

So, what changed? How did Christine become so accepting of herself? It started one day in the church kitchen when she and Lydia were
preparing a meal for the senior citizens' luncheon. Christine and Lydia
were laughing and joking as they cooked and cleaned. Then something
slipped out of Christine's mouth that would change her life. She

confessed as she was putting the chocolate frosting on the cake, "I know it's a sin to like frosting as much as I do, but God's just gonna have to look the other way."

Lydia's response was far from what Christine expected. She looked puzzled and asked, "Why do you think it's a sin to like chocolate frosting?" Christine was so astonished, she couldn't respond. She stammered something about her mom and God hating fat, along with a couple of other reasons.

For the first time, Christine was challenged to consider that God wasn't as concerned about her losing weight as her mother was. Christine's real sin wasn't liking chocolate; it was turning to food for needs that only God could meet. Through developing a more personal relationship with God, she discovered that she was missing out on much courage, strength, and intimacy because of her fear that God rejected her body (as everybody else in her life did). Once she saw herself as fully accepted by God even if she gained 50 pounds, she started to see her body differently.

As a result of growing closer to God, Christine has a new desire to care more for the body He gave her. But she is doing that in a totally different way than she did in the past. She isn't going on some kind of crash diet. Actually, she found a prayer-walking partner in Lydia, and together they walk around the church and neighborhood three times a week praying for their families and their community.

Christine is also making better choices about the food she consumes. She started drinking water before, during, and after her meals. She doesn't deny herself chocolate; rather, she relies on God to help her not to overindulge. Even when she eats too much chocolate, she knows that God is on her side.

Christine is losing weight ever so slowly. The best thing is that she is doing it in the freedom of acceptance by Christ and the power of His love.

The truth: It is not a sin to be overweight. The real sin for many heavy (as well as skinny) people is turning to food (or other substances) to meet needs only God can meet.

🌱 Check yourself:
Do you think God considers your weight when it comes to His love for you?

Lie Six: I must compete with other women
and look as good as they do.
Cindy was packing for the Holy Land tour she was going on with her church. Her thoughts automatically turned to the best dressers from the group. She speculated about what clothes these women would wear and tried to gauge what to take based on how she would look compared to them, rather than what would be most comfortable and wrinkle the least.

I'm 30 and I have never been in a serious
relationship with a man. I'm sure that my
looks have everything to do with that.

Have you ever done the same thing? When you think about what to wear, do you think, *What will the other women be wearing?* Are there women you want to outdress, or do you at least try to dress up to their standards?

You don't achieve self-worth by looking as good as or better than other women. Those who struggle in this area often notice only the women who are more attractive than they are. The habit only leads them to bring to light more body flaws. There will always be women who are prettier or less attractive than you are. That is a given. When you accept this reality, you will be free to think about more important things.

The truth: You will always be the loser when you compete with other women in the beauty arena.

> ❦ Check yourself:
> Do you believe that you are more attractive than some women and less attractive than others?

Lie Seven: My body is who I am.
When did Adam's body come to life? Not the instant it was created. It was lifeless until God breathed into his nostrils the breath of life. Will your body last forever? No, but you will exist eternally either in heaven or hell, depending on whether you receive God's free gift of salvation through Jesus Christ.

I like to think of our bodies as the garage for our souls, where we are parked temporarily while we live on this earth. The health, appearance, and abilities of our bodies affect what we do on this earth, but they are not all of who we are. They are significant to us for our time on earth, but will not last for eternity.

The truth: Your body is part of who you are, but not completely who you are.

> ❦ Check yourself: Do you recognize that you exist in far-reaching ways beyond your body?

Read over your answers and check yourself. Each question that you answer no to indicates that you believe a lie about yourself. Write down the truth in contrast to the lie and put the list somewhere you will see it often (taped to the bathroom mirror, sitting on your dresser, on your car dashboard). Each time you read the truth, ask God to help you believe it.

God's Secret Wisdom

The world says that which can be measured and observed is what gives you value. If the way you look is consistent with the world's view of beauty, then you are considered valuable. But as you saw in Romans 12:1–2, you must be transformed from the world's thinking. The Holy Spirit shows you God's will and gives you God's power when you turn away from the world's pattern. The Holy Spirit does an invisible work that transforms your body image.

> We do, however, speak a message of wisdom among the
> mature, but not the wisdom of this age or of the rulers of this
> age, who are coming to nothing. No, we speak of God's secret
> wisdom, a wisdom that has been hidden and that God destined
> for our glory before time began. None of the rulers of this age
> understood it, for if they had, they would not have crucified the
> Lord of glory. (1 Corinthians 2:6–8)

The wisdom of this age says that you are not worthy unless you look like you are 23 and have large, perky breasts and no body fat. This is not very wise when you consider that our bodies weren't created to have that shape, and most of us eventually live past the age of 23. The majority of the actresses and models who do look like that are abusing their bodies through surgery and starvation. God's secret wisdom is that *every body is beautiful!*

> 🌱 What is the wisdom of this age when it comes to body image?

> 🌱 What is God's secret wisdom?

> 🌱 How many models, movie stars, and advertisers of this age who promote the "perfect body" center their lives on Jesus Christ? Can they possess real wisdom if they don't?

Each of us is unique and special. We may not win the approval of the world for how we look, but true wisdom comes from experiencing the reality that most of what the world offers is untrue. God tells you that you can have peace in your soul no matter what your body looks like.

The world offers you peace if you look a certain way. Does that peace ever come? Have you ever found true, deep, and spiritual peace when you looked your best? Are Hollywood filmmakers, advertisers, and the fashion industry centered on a meaningful relationship with God when they feed us beliefs about what it means to be beautiful? True beauty is experienced as you bask in the center of God's love and care for you—all of you—spirit, body, and soul.

Putting It into Practice

> 🌱 Write down three negative statements you make about your body. Now rewrite them as positive statements by using some of the information in this chapter.

Here's what Laurie wrote in her journal:

1. My scars are ugly and I'm disfigured.
2. My stomach is too round.
3. My varicose veins are hideous.

It was difficult for her to be more realistic, but when she was, she wrote:

1. I am not happy that I had to have a mastectomy, but I'm glad that it was successful in getting rid of my cancer. I will accept it when my husband tells me I am just as sexy to him now as before.
2. Most women have an extra layer of fat across their abdomens. My stomach is here to stay.
3. My veins have gotten worse since I had cancer. I can look at them and celebrate that I am alive!

In a *Guideposts* magazine story, Faye Angus wrote about how she guided her children to have prayer time at the dinner table. She saw this as a time for her children to learn to be comfortable about praying out loud, develop the gift of gratefulness, and speak freely with God. She wrote:

One evening when shepherd's pie, the children's favorite, was on the table, six-year-old Ian enthusiastically volunteered to say the blessing. After he had duly thanked God for the food and the highlights of his day, he paused and then added, "And thank You, God, for the nice little boy You gave this family."

"Nice little boy!" I gasped. "Where?"

"Right here," he grinned, pointing to himself. "I was thanking God for me!"

Doing the dishes later that night, I thought, the boy has a point. We all come tagged with the designer label: "Individually

Crafted with the Compliments of Your Creator." Suddenly I was overwhelmed. Why, in all my years of thanksgiving, I had never ever thanked God for me! Hands dripping wet with suds, eyes spilling tears of wonder, then and there I quietly said, "Thank You, God, for all the workmanship You put into making me!"[2]

Why not follow the example of a six-year-old and thank God for making you?

Discussion Questions

1. How do you have to treat the world's way of thinking about body image if you are going to be transformed into God's way of thinking about your body? (See Romans 12:1–2.)

2. Which of the seven lies do you struggle with most often?

3. Do you struggle to see that God accepts and loves you even if you are overweight and eat compulsively?

4. If we can't all look like movie stars, what should we strive for in our appearance?

5. Why is it magical thinking to believe that if we looked better, our problems would go away?

6. How does the Holy Spirit work to transform your body image?

CHAPTER FIVE

Every Woman Needs to Know She's Beautiful

When you don't like your body, thoughts and feelings of contempt pour over you. You look down at your stomach in the shower and your whole being cringes in shame. You are overcome by disgust and hopelessness. The despair you feel is tightly tied to your sense of who you are. You think that who you are is wrong.

You try to bury your feelings, but they materialize throughout your day. As you finish your last bite at lunch and notice that your waistband is tight, you berate yourself a little more. When you're alone at home and all you can think about is the half-gallon of your favorite ice cream in the freezer, you say, "Why deny myself? My stomach is fat and ugly anyway."

Most women experience these feelings as mild shame, and they are able to function when not distracted by occasional negative thoughts.

But others are trapped in "Bodyhateville" perpetually. They are overcome by guilt, shame, disgust, hopelessness, and anger with each bite of food they put into their mouth. Every glance in the mirror and each person who looks at them reflect reproach and condemnation. Such feelings can crush your spirit. Negative feelings about your body hinder you from receiving the life God wants for you.

Read the following scriptures from Proverbs and answer the questions with these verses in mind.

A happy heart makes the face cheerful, but heartache crushes the spirit. (Proverbs 15:13)

A cheerful heart is good medicine, but a crushed spirit dries up the bones. (Proverbs 17:22)

A man's spirit sustains him in sickness, but a crushed spirit who can bear? (Proverbs 18:14)

The lamp of the LORD searches the spirit of a man; it searches out his inmost being. (Proverbs 20:27)

🌱 How much damage can negative feelings (a crushed spirit) cause in your life?

🌱 Why is it important to address these negative feelings rather than push them away?

Women are emotional creatures. We are usually much more in touch with our feelings than our male counterparts. This is something women like about themselves—that they can identify their feelings and express them to others. A woman's ability to be sensitive to her own and others' feelings brings a positive aspect to her relationships.

The emotional nature of women is highlighted at the central point in history, during Jesus' journey to the cross. Even though Jewish law forbade showing compassion for condemned prisoners, a group of women caught sight of their Savior being brutalized and responded by weeping (Luke 23:27).

Henry Gariepy writes, "With all the record of opposition to Jesus, there is no instance written of in which a woman opposed Christ. No women ever forsook, betrayed, or in any way expressed enmity against Christ. Rather they followed Him, opened to Him their homes and hearts, bathed His feet with their tears, anointed His head with perfume, and now, as men dragged Him to His death, they showed the compassion of their sorrow and wept for Him on His way to martyrdom."[1]

Women can be proud of their emotionally sensitive natures. It is a God-given gift and capacity. This compassion was appropriate for Christ's circumstances on the cross, and in the midst of it, Jesus acknowledged the emotional state of the women. He made the longest recorded statement on His journey to the cross in His address to these precious women:

> Jesus turned and said to them, "Daughters of Jerusalem, do not
> weep for me; weep for yourselves and for your children. For the
> time will come when you will say, 'Blessed are the barren
> women, the wombs that never bore and the breasts that never
> nursed!' Then 'they will say to the mountains, "Fall on us!" and
> to the hills, "Cover us!" ' For if men do these things when the
> tree is green, what will happen when it is dry?" (Luke 23:28–31)

✿ What did Jesus instruct the women to do in this passage?

Jesus didn't scold them for weeping, He merely told them that what they were weeping about was a waste of their time. It was only natural for them to weep. Their Leader, Friend, Healer, and Guide was being brutally battered. This was indeed a sad scene.

But the truth is that this ugly event did not take into account the spiritual reality that God was in control. Jesus' barbaric death was necessary and it fulfilled God's plan. If the women had understood what was actually happening, they wouldn't have needed tears of sorrow. Jesus went on to tell them what they should weep about. They did need to weep because their whole city and temple would be destroyed. That prophecy was fulfilled in A.D. 70.

I think Jesus says something similar to you and me. "Don't weep (feel negative emotions) about your physical body that God gave to you for your earthly existence and which will not last for eternity. Weep (feel negative emotions) about issues that are of true consequence. Weep for the unsaved, for the hurting and confused. You are wasting your tears weeping about your body."

How Women Deal with Negative Feelings

Identifying feelings can bog women down when they don't know what to do with them. When it comes to negative feelings about their bodies, women usually respond in one of two ways: They either try to stuff their feelings, or they try to change their feelings by changing their bodies. Neither brings peace and harmony to their emotions.

Marjorie stuffs her feelings. She is overweight because she gained about 20 pounds with each of her three children. She would need to lose 60 pounds to get back down to her pre-pregnancy weight (a weight she would love to weigh now, but at the time thought was too heavy). Since the birth of her first child, Marjorie has been stuffing her feelings of dislike for her body. The year after her child's birth, she told herself that the extra weight was normal since she was nursing. She tried to convince herself that it didn't bother her. The few comments that her husband made about her weight made her angry. She thought that he was an insensitive man who didn't know what it was like for a woman having babies.

A few times she agreed to a new exercise program with a neighbor, but she did it more for the fellowship than for her health. When it rained or was too hot or too cold and the exercise dates fizzled out, she discovered different ways to fellowship. She had her friends over for dessert and coffee.

Marjorie didn't let herself feel ugly, fat, and unhealthy for long. She quickly changed her emotions by stuffing them away. If you had asked her directly, "How do you feel about your body?" she would have responded, "I feel great. I can eat all the ice cream I want without guilt." The truth is, she had a great deal of guilt. In fact, she was overwhelmed with guilt, low self-esteem, and emptiness. She secretly hated skinny people and couldn't trust them or anything they said. She covered all these negative feelings with her addictions to food, decorating, and television.

I've tried about everything, but there is no
way to change the shape of my thunder thighs.
Running just makes them bigger!

While Marjorie appeared indifferent to any negative feelings about her body, Jana was obsessed with negative feelings almost 24 hours a day. She couldn't have one mellow moment without thinking about how ugly a certain part of her body was. It didn't help that she was a ballerina by profession and danced in front of a mirror while teaching and practicing. The mirror was a living nightmare, haunting her throughout the day. Several times a day she was so overwhelmed by the image she saw that she lost concentration and had to work extra hard to get back on task.

Can you imagine feeling constantly repulsed by the image you saw in the mirror eight hours a day? Jana couldn't escape it. Even while driving from work to the dance studio where she taught, she was confronted by the rearview mirror. Her whole life centered on acknowledging, resisting, and being tormented by debilitating and negative feelings. She felt bad, but it was so much easier for her to hate her body than to acknowledge her hurt and anger toward the important people in her life.

The Power of Emotions

Emotions are a very powerful impetus in your life. Your emotions may not be driving you to the same extremes as Marjorie's or Jana's. You may be somewhere in between. Just as emotions wield a strong negative power, when they are based on truth they become powerful sources of energy and life. I like this description of emotions by Flora Slosson Wuellner:

> No matter how distorted and hurtful our powers within, they were originally created from the divine source, and they hold the potentiality for the unique and beautiful. In their healing, they are not wiped out or destroyed, for nothing in God's creation can ultimately be destroyed. Rather, they are restored to their original, intended power of gifted creativity.

Our fear, when healed, becomes intuitive, empathetic compassion and sensitivity toward others.

Our destructive anger, when healed, becomes a passion, a hunger and thirst for justice and righteousness.

Our perfectionism, our compulsion to organize and dominate, when healed, becomes released, joyous power to build and create.

Our inertia and our withdrawals, when healed, become increasing powers of peace and integrity.

Our possessiveness, our jealousies, and our physical addictions, when healed, become growing released powers to become lovers and healers of the world around us.[2]

🌿 Are you willing to let God heal your negative emotions?

🌿 How have your negative emotions robbed you in this life?

In a sense, you must give consent to God for the healing of emotions to begin. He longs to heal you; He promises to heal you. Wuellner says, "But God's full healing seems to wait for our longing and consent. Is this because we are not helpless puppets but created to be children, heirs, spouses, partners, cocreators with God, our free consent a crucial part of the creative wisdom of gravity?"[3]

When the overwhelming feelings of a negative body image are healed, they turn into wonder and awe at the body God gave each of us. While we respect the limitations our bodies may have compared to others, we value every muscle that we have and every movement we are blessed to make. We turn self-hate into praise for the Creator who made us.

Truth Heals Your Emotions

You've already laid the groundwork in the previous chapters for healing your emotions. From the Bible you have been digging out the truth of who you are and why God made you. When you believe this truth, it will positively affect your feelings. Again, you do not have direct control over your feelings. You do have direct control over how you think and what you do.

My dad told me that guys won't marry fat girls.

It is similar to how your heart functions in your body. Your heart works on an automatic response system. It started beating when you were only a few days past conception and won't stop until physical limitations completely inhibit its ability to operate. In your day-to-day existence, you do not have direct control over your heartbeat. You can take a short jog, and it will beat a little faster. You can rest, and it will slow down. You simply can't tell your heart how and when to beat. Yet you do have some control over the health of your heart through diet and exercise.

It is the same with your feelings. They are automatic responses to what we think about our circumstances. We do not change our feelings by simply saying, "I don't feel that way." However, we can control our feelings by controlling how we think.

If you are searching for emotional freedom from negative feelings about your body, you need to discover how to address your feelings in a healthy way. The following is a guide for dealing with your feelings.

Step One: Identify your feelings. Although Marjorie (the mother of three) appears the healthiest of our previous two examples, actually

Jana (the ballerina) is closer to healing from her emotional deficiencies. Marjorie totally ignores her feelings. She stuffs them down deep by piling on activities and an "I couldn't care less about looking good" attitude in an attempt to keep her feelings in the grave. Jana is totally obsessed with and overcome by negative feelings. However, she will more likely recognize that she needs help handling her negative feelings because they aren't being buried.

Our negative feelings signal that something is wrong. All feelings are real, but not all feelings are true. For instance, you may feel ugly, disgusting, and worthless. Those are real feelings. But you are God's beloved creation, and as such, you are beautiful, appealing, and worth more than gold. You first have to be able to identify your feelings before you can discover the truth that will change your feelings.

❦ Write down any negative feelings you can identify that describe how you feel about your body right now. Here are some to get you started, but you may have others:

angry	anxious	hopeless	sad	embarrassed
tense	worried	gloomy	ashamed	guilty
discouraged	unhappy	repulsive	vain	self-effacing
arrogant	lowly	gross	hideous	forbidding
self-conscious	disgusted	dejected	arrogant	ugly

❦ Now list any positive feelings you can identify that describe how you feel about your body. Here are some examples:

proud	content	satisfied	happy	joyful
in awe	elated	confident	elegant	expectant
positive	pleased	humble	fulfilled	gratified
magnificent	comfortable	delighted	relaxed	undisturbed
whole	decent	beautiful	gorgeous	self-assured

❦ Did you have more negative or more positive feelings?

❦ Read over the positive feelings list. Are those feelings you want to have about your body?

❦ In chapter one you did a chronological survey of memories you have about your body. Refer to that exercise and list beside each memory any feelings you attach to that memory. You can use the feelings listed above or any other feelings that come to mind.

❦ Do you see any correlation between how you feel about your body today and how you have felt about your body throughout your life?

Often when you have a negative body image, it is caused by feelings from the past as well as the present. Negative feelings can haunt you for years unless you learn to speak the truth to them and dispel their negative influence.

When my children were awakened by nightmares in the middle of the night, I would ask them to tell me what they had dreamed. They didn't want to tell me because their dreams frightened them so much; they just wanted to sleep in my bed and forget their awful dreams. I wanted them to tell me their dreams so they could be resolved. I would explain that their nightmares were more likely to go away if they described them.

In the same way, it's healing for women with negative body images and bad feelings from the past to talk about them. Otherwise, the feelings deceive you into believing lies about yourself. The process of sharing those negative feelings and experiences with someone else is a first step in resolving them.

Marybeth, the 49-year-old who refused to be a model in the church fashion show, had hated her body since she was four years old when her stepfather began molesting her. She remembered feeling dirty and ugly, and she just wanted to disappear. These are the same feelings she had when she was asked to be a model for the fashion show. Throughout her life, she carried those negative feelings, never enjoying sex because she was so self-conscious and guilt ridden about her body. She was driven to wear the latest fashions so she could attempt to cover her perceived ugliness.

In order for Marybeth to heal the negative feelings she carried, she needed to deal with her sexual abuse. She needed to feel legitimate anger at her stepfather rather than at herself, and she needed to forgive him to experience freedom in her emotions.

Forgiveness of Others Is the Antidote to Negative Feelings

Every woman reading this book has been hurt in some way by another person. Most of you can think of a specific instance when a person's words or actions left you despising your body. God's direction for healing from those negative feelings is through forgiveness, not through having the perfect body. Whether it's your mother who embarrassed you about your weight, your ex-husband who rejected you, your brother who teased you incessantly, or a stranger who raped you, you will not be free of negative emotions unless you let God heal you through forgiveness.

If the person who has hurt you the most is dead, unwilling to talk to you about what happened, or a stranger, you can still work through the process of forgiveness. Jesus died for the sins of every person who has been born, yet not every one will be reconciled to Him. We are reconciled with Jesus and fully receive His forgiveness only when we admit our sin and accept His free gift of salvation.

It is the same with our human relationships. Forgiveness does not necessarily include reconciliation. We need to fully forgive, even when there is no promise of being reconciled. I encourage you to work through the stages of forgiveness with any person listed in your chronological survey who has hurt you. If you need help, ask your pastor or a mature woman at your church to encourage you through this process. You won't be sorry!

Good Feelings Are Good!

Balance is the key to positive feelings about your body. Is it okay for a woman to feel magnificent, delighted, beautiful, gorgeous, or elegant? You may wonder if you are a bad Christian if you feel that way about yourself. Personally, I would have loved to hear Marjorie say she felt beautiful, delighted, gorgeous, and elegant (plus the rest of the positive list from page 97), even while she was 60 pounds overweight.

I knew it was possible for her to feel that way. I also knew that if she felt that way, she would take better care of the body she is so blessed to have. When her thoughts and feelings got in balance, her behaviors would follow. She might need some help from a dietitian or friend, but her desire to lose weight would develop out of her belief in and confidence about the value of her body.

I asked Marjorie to say loudly, "I'm drop-dead gorgeous to God," three times. She rolled her eyes and looked at me as if I were crazy, but she obediently complied. Each time I encouraged her to say it a little louder. By the end, she was laughing and said, "That actually made me feel better." It was as if a cloud had been lifted. After being encouraged to accept how God wants her to feel about her body, the lock on her stuffed feelings of shame, betrayal, and hurt sprang open.

Step Two: Identify the ways your negative feelings are harming you. Once Marjorie felt her negative feelings, she caught up to Jana, who was completely obsessed by hers. Both were asked to spell out just what their negative feelings were costing them.

Marjorie made a list of the effects her negative feelings had on her life. She recognized how she had become prejudiced against skinny people and disliked them without even knowing them. She also took note of the poor eating habits she had established and encouraged in her children. Her "I don't care" attitude had been hurtful not just to her personally, but also to others. She made the connection to her addictions to television, food, and shopping. She saw them as a distraction or escape to make her feel better.

Jana's list wasn't so hard to do. She didn't discover anything new as she wrote. She was already very aware of the prison she lived in every day. She listed the parties she had dressed for and then skipped because her stomach stuck out too far. She thought of all the young girls in her dance class that she could have built relationships with and mentored. But she had been too busy obsessing about her body to make a connection with them.

Jana knew she would have more confidence as a ballerina if she could be more focused on her dancing and less self-conscious about her body. Although she was acceptable as a dancer, she realized that her negative feelings were holding her back.

🌱 How are your feelings about your body hurting you?

Step Three: Decide to believe the truth. Marjorie and Jana came to the same conclusion after surveying their feelings about their bodies.

They both decided they were wasting time and so much of their lives by either obsessing over or ignoring their feelings. This became the impetus to put the truths they had been learning to work for them.

Each of them wrote out scriptures that reminded them how God wanted them to think about their bodies. Beside each scripture they wrote the truth about how God sees them and their bodies. Every time Marjorie was tempted to watch television, she read through the cards. Jana kept her cards in her bag and went over them during her breaks. She also recorded them on a tape to listen to in her car. Both were amazed at how different they felt after doing this for only one day.

Marjorie couldn't believe how often she felt bad about herself. She hadn't been aware of how strong her negative feelings were. It surprised her to find out that many of her decisions to watch television, eat, and shop were an effort to stuff down her feelings.

The hardest area to resist was food. It had a strong hold on her, and it was easy to indulge while she was home alone. She ended up putting stop signs on her refrigerator and the cabinet where the cookies were kept. A few times she ate the cookies anyway. She had a heart-to-heart talk with herself, facing up to the real reason she wanted those cookies so much.

I wonder how I can be so organized, so disciplined, so in control of most of my life, yet fail so miserably when it comes to my weight.

Marjorie discovered that emptiness was an emotion she most often filled with food. As she thought about that, she discovered some of the lies she had believed about herself. She felt empty as a stay-at-home mom. She felt angry that she did not have as much money as the two-income families in her neighborhood. She criticized herself for not being able to afford to take the family out to dinner like everyone who lived around her.

The whole neighborhood emptied out during the workweek. Marjorie was left alone with her dog, Georgie, and all she had to do was watch television and eat, in between doing the chores of running a household. When Marjorie started tuning in to her feelings, she discovered that she didn't believe she was of much value to others since she stayed at home with her children and didn't get a paycheck. But God's Word reminded her that her worth was much more than rubies (Proverbs 31:10). She decided to start listening to God and cherish the moments she could enjoy with her children.

Jana's thinking also needed a major overhaul. She recognized the immensity of the work ahead. She had drilled into her head so many lies about herself that she couldn't expect instant success. She needed to harness all the discipline she had used to shape herself into a prima ballerina. She knew that if she didn't do something, she would lose everything she had worked so tirelessly to build.

Jana found an accountability partner, a woman who knew nothing about dancing in public but everything about dancing with God. She knew how to let God have control of her mind so she could live in the truth.

Jana also kept up with her discipline of listening to the tape she'd made and reading over those truths during her breaks. She would journal each night about her negative and positive feelings about her body. After six months, she took an evening to read through her journal. What she discovered encouraged and surprised her. She could see how her accounts of negative feelings toward her body were getting shorter and those of her positive feelings were getting longer. This was a big breakthrough for Jana.

Step Four: Enjoy how your body feels. Most women are so hung up on how their bodies look, they miss out on how their bodies feel. God designed our bodies to give us pleasure. You need to replace your negative body feelings—based on shame, anger, and disgust about how you look—with positive pleasures from how your body senses the world around you.

Stop right now and softly rub your hands together. How does that feel? Are your hands soft and warm? Do you know that you have more nerve endings in your fingertips? Now rub your hands over your forearm. How does that feel? It is a different sensation because you don't have as many nerve endings on your forearm.

You are probably familiar with the saying, "Stop and smell the roses." Too many women don't stop and smell the roses—recognizing the wonder of their bodies. Sometimes it takes being confronted with a potentially fatal disease for a woman to begin to appreciate her body. Your body is an amazing combination of traits conceived by an extremely creative God. We miss out on enjoying and appreciating our bodies when we fail to recognize that fact.

Both Jana and Marjorie were challenged to get more in touch with their body sensations every day. Each was told to literally stop and smell the roses, engaging her sense of smell to bring positive feelings about her body.

You too need to tune in to the world around you through your body's amazing senses. Make special efforts to experience your sense of touch. Touch children, hug your friends, get a massage, shake hands, all the time being conscious of your body's enjoyment of pleasure. Cultivate your senses of smell, taste, touch, sight, and hearing.

When you are on a binge-eating craze, you don't taste, see, or smell your food. Get some chocolate ice cream (or your favorite flavor). Eat it slowly. Feel the coolness, the smooth texture, and don't miss the taste of your ice-cream cone. When you eat this way, you will eat more slowly and with more satisfaction. You won't be eating to stuff your feelings but to enjoy your feelings. Praise God for the wonder of ice cream as you eat.

Being aware of your body's sensations is part of your connection to other people. When we meet new people, we often shake hands. We hug relatives we haven't seen in a while. Giving a hug is a sign of the deeper connection that we make with them.

Try one of the following activities to increase your awareness of your physical feelings:

1. Take time to enjoy a beautiful sunrise or sunset. Let your eyes enjoy the vision of this colorful masterpiece.

2. Make a special effort to touch objects and appropriately touch people in a 24-hour period. As you sit down at your desk, run your hand across the smooth wood. Touch flowers and pets, give more hugs, take time to feel the wonder of your world.

3. Discipline yourself to slowly chew every bite you put into your mouth. Think of a special food that you enjoy. Take a certain amount of time to eat it, savoring the taste.

4. Listen to the sounds of nature in a park near your house. Tune in to the birds chirping, the wind blowing, the water running. Try to identify as many sounds as you can.

5. Celebrate your sense of smell. Go to a flower garden and take in the scent of each bloom.

Step Five: Eliminate body shame and sexual shame. Deep beneath Jana's shame about her body was a secret she kept carefully hidden. She never wanted to admit to herself or anyone else what happened to her the summer she was 15 and visiting her father at his home several states away. Her father worked during the day, and she was left to hang out with the neighborhood kids whom she had never met before. They were a little faster than the crowd she spent time with at home. She turned down several invitations to parties at night, but she felt safe to play pool or hang out at the home of a neighbor, Stacy.

At age 54, I pretty much have accepted what I have, although I could stand to lose five pounds.

One day, near the end of the summer, Tony came to the house. Jana was instantly attracted to this good-looking guy. After a game of pool, they sat down together on the couch in Stacy's basement. Jana didn't notice it at the time, but as if on cue, all the other kids disappeared from the basement. She was alone with Tony. He continued flirting with her. She felt fine with this, but when he pushed her to fool around more, she began to feel uncomfortable. Tony was very good at getting what he wanted, and without totally realizing what was happening, Jana became a victim of date rape in a few short minutes.

After he was finished, Tony went over to the pool table and invited her to play a game. When she was able to pull herself together, she ran to her father's house without looking at anyone. There was no one home, so she ran to the bathroom and showered for an hour. She was leaving in two days, and she asked her father to let her spend the last two nights at her grandmother's house.

Jana wanted to call her mom, but she knew how much it made her dad mad when she called her on his visitations. By the time she got home, she didn't even tell her mom. She found her best escape in pretending she had never laid eyes on Tony. On a good day, she couldn't even remember his name when she tried.

There are so many women like Jana and Marybeth whose negative feelings about their bodies are intertwined with unwanted sexual experiences, or shameful sexual activities in which they participated. It is necessary for women to be healed from their sexual shame in order to be at peace with their bodies. A great number of women with eating disorders have been sexually abused. A strong correlation exists between mistreating your body with food, bingeing, purging, and so on, and having an emotional vault deep inside filled with sexual shame.

Like Marybeth and Jana, you may have negative feelings about your body as the result of sexual abuse. If so, you need to heal from that wound through forgiveness; otherwise you remain a victim. If your negative feelings about your body are associated with sexual sin from the past, you need to receive God's cleansing through forgiveness.

If we confess our sins, he is faithful and just and will forgive us our sins and purify us from all unrighteousness. (1 John 1:9)

❦ What is our part in being forgiven for past and present sins?

❦ What does God do when we confess?

Part of learning to let go of negative feelings about your body is receiving God's forgiveness. If you are trapped in the pit of shame and disgrace because of sexual experiences you've had, God invites you to be cleansed. I love the way He describes what actually happens when He forgives us. He grants us a clean slate. He cleanses us from the stain of sin. We are made new. You don't have to feel defiled by sexual shame and sin. You can be completely clean.

Step Six: Feel confident in your body. The payoff to all that hard work is feeling confident in the body you live in. So what if your tummy is a little round? You can still work out three times a week. You can lift and bend and perform all the movements necessary to do your laundry, walk the dog, or fly a kite. Your body is amazing! When you know that, you'll feel different. You'll still have a round tummy, but you'll have a different response to it. It won't make you feel disgusted, ashamed, or unworthy. It's a part of being human. It's a fact of life.

Your feelings will change when you get the right thoughts in your mind. The choice is yours. You can feel confident or contemptible. Your feelings are based on what you think. Your focus changes from how you want to look to how you want to feel about how you look. Feeling good inside your body is evidence of a healthy body image.

A few years ago, I attended a mother-son campout. It was a wonderful weekend. My friend Tammy, who invited me, had told me about the ropes course the moms would be asked to do. We were supposed to climb up a telephone pole, then walk across another telephone pole and a flimsy wire before we came to a platform. From there we had to take a zip line to the ground. She told me it wasn't mandatory, but that my son would be proud of me for trying.

As I stood in line, my feet and the palms of my hands literally filled with sweat at the prospect of such a feat. (Did I mention that we wore harnesses attached to ropes that would catch us if we fell?) I put on my helmet and climbed up the pole. As I stood facing the horizontal pole, I thought, *I could jump right now and let the line catch me.* I didn't want to move forward and felt terrified of walking out on that very high and narrow pole.

Rather than give in to my feelings, though, I prayed and asked God to help me get across. I put my trust in Him, not in my own ability. My feelings of utter terror turned into feelings of peace, and I calmly (at least that's the way I remember it now) walked across the pole.

High-climbing stunts may not be for you. But the high-flying experience of confidence in the body you live in is what God has in store. You can become free of your despair. You can live in confidence. You can soar emotionally. Keep your thoughts on God's Word. Accept God's values. Receive God's help. Your emotional well-being can change as a result.

Discussion Questions

1. How can your feelings crush your spirit?

2. Why do some women stuff their feelings?

3. Why do other women obsess over their feelings?

4. Why is what we believe important to changing our feelings?

5. Share an example of how you have experienced inner healing through forgiveness.

6. What are some of the favorite sensations you enjoy with your body?

CHAPTER SIX

Healthier Ever After

*T*his study isn't meant to be a six-week reprieve from self-loathing. My hope is that you will break free from the trap of body hate and genuinely enjoy the wonder of your body for the rest of your life. I long for you to accept the body you live in and have an accurate grasp of its significance for your existence on earth.

It's not as if there is a perfect cure for the disease of body hate. From time to time you may still wish for a flatter stomach, thinner thighs, or a remedy for whatever it is that bothers you most. But you can live free of self-loathing by learning to believe the truth about who you are. God longs for us to be confident women focused on living in and enjoying our bodies, not being enslaved to them.

> Your beauty should not come from outward adornment, such as
> braided hair and the wearing of gold jewelry and fine clothes.
> Instead, it should be that of your inner self, the unfading beauty
> of a gentle and quiet spirit, which is of great worth in God's sight.
> For this is the way the holy women of the past who put their
> hope in God used to make themselves beautiful. (1 Peter 3:3–5)

❧ What does beauty *not* come from?

❧ What is true beauty—beauty that never fades?

My husband's grandfather often told his wife that she was as beautiful as the day he first laid eyes on her. Brian and I stayed with his grandmother the night of his grandfather's funeral. We sat on the bed with her as she reflected on the day he died at home in her arms. She said, "That morning he told me that I looked as beautiful as the day he first met me when I was 16."

Indeed, she was ultimate beauty to him—even with her wrinkles, sparse hair, and thick glasses. Her beauty hadn't faded with the passage of time, but had grown brighter. Her beauty sprang from the loving and caring relationship she shared with him. That relationship had grown even more precious with time.

> *It didn't take me long to figure out that I was a freak. I was born with deformed fingers, and kids were cruel! I don't even try to imagine what it might be like to be pretty. I know I will never be seen that way, so I focus on being smart.*

That's the same way God sees us according to 1 Peter 3:3–5. Our beauty is revealed even in the body flaws we each carry. Our beauty is in a gentle and quiet spirit. When you read the words *gentle* and *quiet,* you might think of a meek and timid person. But you can be loud and outgoing and still be gentle and quiet in your spirit.

A gentle and quiet spirit is exhibited as you place your complete trust in God. When a woman stops struggling to be what everyone else thinks she should be, and instead lets herself enjoy what God wants her to be, she portrays a gentle and quiet spirit. A woman with a gentle and quiet spirit feels assured of her beauty.

Breaking the Chains

Marybeth was challenged to let go of her controlling behaviors in regard to her body. She's the one who refused to be a model for the women's ministry fashion show. After working through her grief and anger and forgiving her stepfather for sexually abusing her, Marybeth needed to face her own sins. One of them was the way she looked at her body. Even though she looked the best she could, she never felt satisfied and confident in her own skin.

She practiced the mind makeover for weeks and weeks, and decided the best way to show she was accepting God's love for her was to attend the women's retreat without wearing makeup the whole morning. She made this decision privately; it was just between herself and God. This is what she wrote about her experience:

God,

I can't believe how completely You have set me free. Me, the one who wouldn't spend one minute in front of women without all my makeup on, went not just the morning, but the whole day without makeup. You know, no one even noticed. I thought for sure everyone would ask me if I was sick or something, but not one person said a thing.

Oh God, forgive me for the years I have wasted hating my body and trying to avoid rejection about how I look. I so over-personalized everything. No one looks at me the way I thought they did. No one was ever as cruel to me about my looks as I was to myself. Thank You for this insight and victory this weekend. It is such a blessing to be loved by a God as wonderful as You. Help me share this with my daughter, Kathy. Sometimes I recognize that she does so many of the same things I used to do.

Paul wrote to the church at Philippi (Philippians 1:6) that he was confident of their spiritual growth. I am confident that as long as you let the truth of God's Word enter fully into your life, you too will become more and more confident in your body. You will grasp the reality of true beauty. You will understand that beauty is about character, not whether your arms wiggle in the wind.

Body Hate Relapse Plan

It takes work to make changes in your thought patterns and feelings. It's too much to expect that you will never need to address this area of your life again just because you finish this book. It is very likely that living in our culture may cause you to struggle to keep negative body stress at a minimum, but the key to succeeding is to be prepared. Here are some suggestions to help you stay on track:

1. Accept that you are not perfect. If you make it your goal to never have a negative thought or feeling about your body again, you are setting yourself up for failure. Be realistic in your expectations.

*In general, I feel okay. But if I think about it, I
know I could tone up everywhere.*

2. Take inventory of your mind. What you keep in your mind is the most important factor in maintaining a healthy body image. For example, you might see an actress your own age who looks like she is much younger and think, *I should try to look that young too.* Are you going to let that thought stay in your mind? Be aware of when these kinds of thoughts enter your mind and address them. You need to take every thought captive in order to attain the emotional, psychological, and spiritual peace you are seeking.

3. Get enough rest for your body. Don't underestimate your need for rest. You can set yourself up for failure when you aren't concerned about how tired you are. Become aware of when you are pushing yourself to do too much.

Often, overeating is related to fatigue. When your body feels sluggish and out of sorts, instead of a nap, you may grab a candy bar for energy. If you get enough rest, though, you will be better able to attend to the issues you face each day. Rest is vital to emotional, spiritual, and physical wellness. You may have to decide to let go of some other things in order to care for your body adequately.

4. Recognize negative feelings and deal with them daily. I've already warned that you will have to deal with the temptation to belittle yourself. Your feelings will sound the alarm; the first time you become aware of self-disgust, take notice. Don't let that negative feeling slide, or it will build up to an endless number of negative feelings and thoughts. Stop yourself right then and there. Examine the feeling, tell God about the feeling, journal about it, and decide to believe His truth about it.

5. Enlist an accountability partner/prayer partner. Do you remember how much Jesus encouraged His disciples to pray to avoid temptation? Prayer is a powerful and effective tool. God promises that when two or more are gathered in His name, He is there with them (Matthew 18:20). Take advantage of this important spiritual reality. Find a prayer partner whom you can call at a particularly bad time. You don't have to pray only about body image; you can pray about other issues as well.

6. Reread this book and complete the exercises. It is very important for you to reread books that have had a particular impact on you. You may think you have received everything a book has to offer after you've read it once. But later you may be at a different place and need to think through some issues again. You may need extra encouragement to let the truth sink into your total being.

7. Don't judge how others look. A sure way to maintain the newer, healthier you is to examine how you look at and talk about others' bodies. When you are less critical of others, you will be less critical of yourself.

When you see the actress who has aged since you saw her last, consider how wonderful it is that she's still getting parts. Think about how great it is that the woman in the wheelchair is able to get around the grocery store the way she can. When you see plus-size models in magazines, consider what a positive trend it is to see images of normal women. Try to see people beyond what is on the outside. Think about people the way God thinks of them: He looks at their hearts.

When my weight started fluctuating in my thirties, I started
a training program for a marathon. It did wonders for my
overall health and fitness, and controlled my weight as well.

8. Don't receive criticism about how you look from others. Many women are in relationships with husbands, mothers, boyfriends, children, coworkers, bosses, girlfriends, and others who criticize their appearance. When you aren't the only one criticizing yourself, it is more difficult to maintain a healthy body image.

If you are in this situation, my heart goes out to you because you are in a painful relationship or relationships. You need the prayers and support of your group to help you. It's easy for me to say, "Don't listen to those who criticize you," but it is much more difficult for you to put it into practice. Make up your mind to resist these negative words with the help of God and your study or prayer group.

9. Recognize the symptoms of relapse. Here is a checklist that will help you recognize the symptoms of relapse before they go too far. Check any questions that are true of you.

_____ Am I getting inadequate rest for my body?

_____ Am I projecting my bad feelings about my body onto others? (I'm sure my friend noticed that I gained 10 pounds, but she is too nice to mention it.)

_____ Am I impatient about the physical results of eating better and exercising?

_____ Am I irritable with others?

_____ Am I feeling depressed about my body?

_____ Am I suffering from self-pity? (Why do my thighs have to be shaped this way?)

_____ Do I think I've got my self-loathing conquered and believe I can handle anything?

_____ Do I agree with others who make self-loathing statements?

_____ Am I being too hard on myself in other areas now, in place of how I used to criticize my body?

_____ Am I ungrateful for the wonder of my body, its senses, complicated structure, and other amazing things?

_____ Do I think I've come too far now to fall back again?

If you checked even one statement, you may be headed for a relapse. Two or more checks mean that you are dangerously close to relapse.

10. Write yourself a letter. In counseling I often ask individuals to write a letter to themselves about a new truth they are learning. It's time to write yourself a letter explaining the truths you've learned about your body. Keep the letter and read it every time you have negative feelings about your body.

Here's what Marybeth wrote:

Dear Marybeth,

God wants you to fully accept that you are beautiful to Him. You are His creation; He made you. You are wonderfully made. Even though your stepfather hurt you in your body and soul, it doesn't change God's creation into something dirty or ugly. When you are feeling dirty, ugly, fat, made wrong, and inadequate, you are believing the lie Satan placed in your mind when you were four years old. You've listened to that lie for so many years, it is hard to stop it, but with the help of the Holy Spirit you can be free.

God has set you free from the lie. You can choose to live in His truth and be free to enjoy the rest of His creation, or you can choose to sink back into the mire and darkness of your miserable thinking. The choice is yours! I know you will make the right one.

I'm proud of how you look, body flaws and all!

Marybeth

🌷 Take some time now to write a letter in your journal.

Tips for Looking Your Best

It is not sinful to think about how you look and to try to look your best. But it is sinful when your appearance becomes your identity. Women can choose two unhealthy responses: One is to put too much emphasis on their appearance, and the other is to ignore how they look entirely.

Paying attention to looks should be important to Christian women. In fact, Paul included some instructions for women about their appearance in his letters to Timothy, in which he explained the doctrines and disciplines of the church: "I also want women to dress modestly, with decency and propriety, not with braided hair or gold or pearls or expensive clothes, but with good deeds, appropriate for women who profess to worship God" (1 Timothy 2:9–10).

❧ Why does God want women to dress modestly?

God wants women to dress modestly and with decency so everything in their lives reveals their reverence for Him. If you've ever searched for a home, you know what it is like to enter the residence of strangers with your Realtor. You can tell a lot about the homeowners by the way they decorate. Workers I've had in my home have mentioned that they can tell I'm a Christian. In your home there are clues to your priorities beyond what you say and how you live.

Likewise, there are clues to your relationship with God in the clothes that you wear. It is important to think about your appearance and what it reveals to the world about your devotion to God.

❧ Describe how you think Christian women should dress.

I don't think Christian women should wear a uniform or look exactly alike. In fact, I think these beauty tips by Audrey Hepburn are very appropriate for Christian women:
- For attractive lips, Speak words of kindness.
- For lovely eyes, Seek out the good in people.

- For a slim figure, Share your food with the hungry.
- For beautiful hair, Let a child run his or her fingers through it once a day.
- For poise, Walk with the knowledge you'll never walk alone.[1]

Since we are on the subject of beauty tips, I share my practical advice about outward beauty in Appendix 1. If you have time, read over that appendix now. If not, go back to it later.

God's Role in Liking the Body You Live In

The number one reason not to berate and mistreat your body is because God is the One who created you. He loves you, and when you love someone you don't want to see her berating herself.

How do you let God be the reason you love your body? Don't feel shame about your body when it comes to your relationship with God. He doesn't look down on you because you have a desire to look nice. In fact, God wants to be your partner in your plan to care for your body. Symeon the New Theologian (A.D. 949–1022) wrote this revealing poem:

> We awaken in Christ's body
> as Christ awakens our bodies,
> and my poor hand is Christ,
> He enters my foot,
> and is infinitely me.
>
> I move my hand,
> and wonderfully
> my hand becomes Christ,
> becomes all of Him

(for God is indivisibly
whole, seamless in His Godhood).

I move my foot, and at once
He appears like a flash
of lightning.

Do my words
seem blasphemous?

Then open your heart to Him and let yourself receive
the one who is opening
to you so deeply.

For if we genuinely love Him,
we wake up inside
Christ's body where all our body, all over,
every most hidden part of it,
is realized in joy as Him,
And He makes us, utterly, real,
And everything that is hurt,
everything that seemed to us dark, harsh, shameful, maimed,
ugly, irreparably damaged,
is in Him transformed
and recognized as whole,
as lovely,
and radiant in His light.

We awaken as the beloved
in every last part of our body.[2]

Discussion Questions

1. What is true beauty according to 1 Peter 3:4–5?

2. What does a gentle and quiet spirit look like in a woman?

3. What steps can you take to guard against relapse?

4. Share practical tips you've found for making over your clothes, makeup, and so on.

5. What is the right perspective about food and how you eat?

6. Read the letter you wrote to yourself about who you are and the truths you've learned about your body.

Practical Makeover Tips

It's time for some practical application regarding the issues we've been discussing. I hope this information is a helpful guide as you make important decisions about caring for your body.

Make Over Your Clothes

Beth began to face the facts. She had spent way too much time, money, and effort on her body. She would never have imagined it before, but when she tallied up her receipts for the year, she discovered that she had spent 25 percent of the family income on clothes, most of them for herself. Financial expert Ron Blue recommends that your family budget include 3 to 4 percent for clothing.[1] Something definitely needed to change.

For Beth, clothing was a very significant issue. What about you? You should have the right kind of clothes for the workplace, church activities, and the social gatherings you attend. There may be times that you'll spend extra money on a special outfit. But ultimately, do you worship God or worship your clothes?

My daughter has learned how to get me to buy something for her—she searches the paper for sales. It is important for me to make sure I get a good bargain on the clothes I buy. I think something in the female chromosome makes women love to get a bargain. It is also a way for me to be a good steward of the money God has entrusted to me. I have many friends who like sales but who wouldn't sacrifice quality in their clothes for a good price. I think that is right for them. The most important thing is that your clothing expenditures are in balance.

Joan's closet looked like that of a schoolgirl who had to wear uniforms. Her uniform was dark-colored sweats. Her whole closet was full of navy and black. She thought she was too fat to wear brighter colors. A step of growth for Joan was going out and buying a colorful outfit that fit her at just the size she was right then. She needed to value herself enough to wear nice clothes.

Take inventory of your closet. In which direction do you need to change? Is God speaking to you about your dedication to clothes? Could you go three months without making a clothing purchase for yourself? Or do you, like Joan, need to pay a little more attention to your wardrobe?

Make Over Your Makeup

Some women choose not to wear makeup as part of their spiritual discipline. They interpret certain scriptures as restricting makeup for women: To wear makeup would be to disobey God's Word. I encourage those women to be faithful to their understanding of Scripture and to do so with joy and gladness. God wants your obedience to be out of love for Him and not from a resentful heart. Your makeup is the beauty of an obedient and loving heart.

For the women who do not interpret Scripture to forbid makeup, I encourage you to wear it wisely. It's not a bad thing to have a makeover at a department store or elsewhere to learn how to apply makeup tastefully. However, be careful that you aren't deceived into thinking you need every product in your makeover. The salesperson's goal is to make you think you need a lot of products to be beautiful because that means more profits for the store.

It is not mandatory for women to wear makeup. If you wear it, make sure that it is not too time-consuming and doesn't interfere with your budget. I use my makeup to protect my skin from the sun. It takes me about five minutes to apply all my makeup. I am a pretty efficient person, but I don't think it should take you more than about 15 minutes to put on your makeup each morning. If it takes you longer, think about steps you can eliminate in your makeup process. You may be wearing too much makeup or be too focused on looking just right.

Beth found she could make a few changes in her makeup. She learned that she could buy a cheaper brand, rather than the department store brand, and get the same results. (Some department store brands also produce a cheaper line. For instance, Lancôme also makes L'Oréal.) She continued to use a few of her favorite things, but got by with eye shadow and mascara from the drugstore.

Joan has never worn much makeup because she didn't want to bother with it. She decided it would be appropriate to protect her skin from sun exposure, so she bought a foundation with sunscreen. She has some blush, eye shadow, and lipstick that she uses for special occasions, but she feels comfortable wearing minimal makeup each day.

Make Over Your Skin Care

Skin care products are a major economic industry in America. Tons of products promise to cure whatever bothers you. It is wise to make a habit of cleaning and moisturizing your skin daily. Don't go for the most expensive products or be deceived by every promise. Experiment until you find a regimen that works for you, your time, and your budget. Use products that help protect your skin from sun damage and that heal your skin. Beth showed Joan how to care for her skin. They are both using the same product line and their skin looks fresh and healthy.

There are numerous nonsurgical ways you can make your skin look younger. I encourage you to think about stewardship as you consider these options. Remember how our mothers tried to motivate us to eat our carrots by reminding us of the hungry children in Africa or China? I sound a little like that when I ask you to think about what good that money could do for needy people today. Is it really worth the expense to look a little better? Would some of that money be better spent elsewhere? I encourage you to pray about how much money you should commit to your skin care and age reduction.

Make Over Your Diet

Okay, I know you hear your mother's voice, or other voices, telling you that you can't eat what you like anymore. Most Americans do eat horribly! Are you one of them? I bet I could give you a Bible quiz and a food quiz and most of you would score higher on the food quiz. Most Americans are very informed about how to eat right. We know which foods to avoid and which to eat lots of, but we don't make the right choices. Why?

There are several reasons. At the same time that we are being indoctrinated about what we *should* eat, we are being bombarded with what we *can* eat. We can find pizza, ice cream, french fries, doughnuts, and pastries on every street corner. They taste good, they're available, and we don't have to think much about it. They offer an easy way to make ourselves happy, if just for a moment. A great deal of our eating is mindlessly pursuing quick fixes.

We establish bad habits that aren't easy to break. It takes discipline to eat right. You must make unpopular choices at restaurants. Others may accuse you of making them feel guilty if you pass up dessert. No one likes to deny herself. Trying to eat food that is good for your body often goes against your natural cravings.

From the first hours after your birth, you learned to equate food with getting your needs met. A newborn's world is centered on eating and sleeping. If the newborn is receiving adequate nourishment, she will sleep and grow properly. It is easy to equate food with feeling better, even when the food makes you feel guilty and sluggish after it is consumed.

If you are overweight, I counsel you not to begin a diet. Rather, think about what your body needs when you make food and exercise decisions. Most obesity in women is the result of a poor body image. Make peace with the body you have right now at the weight you are. Establish in your mind that God loves and accepts you just the way you are, even if you were to gain 100 pounds. When you accept yourself, you will be free to decide how to feed and nourish your body. When you honor and appreciate your body, you will not abuse it through either overeating or with fad diets.

Food Is Important in God's Plan

God went to extreme measures to create a world for Adam and Eve to live in. A big part of that was planting trees in the garden that were good for food and pleasing to the eye (Genesis 2:9). It is necessary to eat. It is fine to eat what you like. God created food to provide the nutrition that our bodies need for fuel, and He also created food for pleasure.

If you find honey, eat just enough—too much of it, and you will vomit. (Proverbs 25:16)

Before and after the Fall, it is clear that God intended food for both nourishment and pleasure. Jesus ate with His disciples and served them bread and fish after His resurrection (John 21:13). He longs to give us the right to eat of the Tree of Life (Revelation 22:14), where we can enjoy the wedding supper of the Lamb (Revelation 19:9). So how does food move so far from being an enjoyable experience to being the worst enemy or best friend of some?

Food, just like every other aspect of our existence on earth, was transformed after the Fall. Food became a major factor in the consequences of the curse, since food would be difficult to cultivate because of thorns and thistles. Today researchers and food specialists have solved these production problems in some parts of the world. Yet the overabundance of food creates a new problem: overindulgence—using food to solve emotional problems. The curse still plagues us today. In America we are tormented with too many food choices.

Many women reading this book may have a legitimate need to lose weight. This is not a weight-loss book, so you may wish to get more specific guidance from a dietitian or nutritionist. Some women are uneducated about nutrition. Many would be surprised to find that there are ways to prepare food and enjoy it while consuming more vitamins and minerals, fewer empty calories, and less fat. When you make peace with your body, you will naturally want to treat your body well.

Many women struggle to eat correctly because they have an unrealistic target weight in mind. It is not wise to go on a diet to lose a certain number of pounds. I recommend that women learn what their bodies should weigh in order to be healthy, then learn how to eat and exercise to get there—even if it takes years to achieve the goal weight. You can consult with your physician or dietitian to determine what is a healthy weight range for you, but one tool you can use as a starting point is the body mass index (BMI).[2]

Here is a three-step process to determine your BMI.

1. Multiply your weight in pounds by 703.

2. Divide that number by your height in inches.

3. Divide that number by your height in inches again. The answer is your BMI.

Marybeth's BMI is 24.2.

1. She weighs 150 pounds x 703 = 105,450.

2. She is 66 inches tall, so 105,450 divided by 66 = 1597.7272.

3. 1597.7272 divided by 66 again = 24.2 BMI.

The National Institutes of Health Web site says an adult woman's BMI should be between 18.5 and 24.9 to be in the healthy range.

Suggested Eating Plan

If you are deciding to eat better, I recommend that you choose a food plan that allows you to eat normal food from the grocery store and make real-life decisions in restaurants. Many people are successful at losing weight on special and bizarre diets, but they rarely keep the weight off. Many of these diets abuse the body.

The right motivation for changing your diet is to take better care of your body, not to look better for your high school reunion. Don't make dietary changes that may help you lose weight but are harmful to you.

People who make small, gradual changes are often more successful in the long run than those who make sudden major changes. One simple plan is to drink water before, during, and after each meal and walk two miles each day. Try this for one month and discover what a difference these two simple changes make. As it is with our spiritual lives, it's all about the cleansing (drinking water) and having a consistent walk.

Good Eaters Take Notice

Some people exhibit an eating disorder that isn't noticed by their doctors or friends. Some women eat so perfectly that their blood work reveals a completely healthy specimen, yet their spirits are not free. These women are overcommitted to fitness and wellness to the exclusion of spiritual well-being. Do you place your trust in your good eating and exercise habits, and not in God's provision and care for you? If so, you may need to work a little more on your eating habits by loosening up a bit. You should be free to have a piece of birthday cake or other dessert once in a while.

Here are some suggestions to establish healthy eating patterns:

1. Schedule three meals a day at regular times. Don't skip meals.
2. Try to eat with your family at the kitchen table as often as possible. If you are single, invite others to eat with you at your kitchen table.
3. Don't nibble during meal preparation.
4. When you eat, concentrate on experiencing your food, its texture, smell, and taste, and not shoveling everything into your mouth.
5. Eat slowly; put your fork down between bites.
6. Drink half your body weight in ounces of fresh water daily. For example, if you weigh 120 pounds, you should drink about 60 ounces of water each day.
7. Enjoy pleasant music and conversation during your meals.
8. Recognize that it is normal to feel full after a meal and your belt or waistband will feel a little tighter. Don't condemn yourself for eating and enjoying your meal.
9. Don't keep a record of forbidden foods. You should include desserts and foods you like (in proper proportion) in your regular eating schedule.
10. Don't eat in the car, bus, bedroom, or bathroom, at the kitchen sink, or on the run. Make a point of sitting down and enjoying your food.

11. Don't try to lose weight too fast. Losing one to two pounds a week is healthier for your body.
12. Eat fewer fatty foods and simple sugars.
13. Eat more fresh fruits, vegetables, and whole grains.
14. Engage in moderate physical activity.
15. Avoid fast food restaurants except for the occasional splurge.

Make Over Your Exercise

Do you feel another lecture coming on? Yes, we all need to exercise. Americans are too sedentary. One thing I want to make clear to you: I hate to exercise. In spite of that fact, I have been exercising three times a week since 1995.

Some people find that after committing to exercise, they start to like it. Not me. I hate sweating. I can't wait to finish. I love to check it off my list. I never throw in an extra day just for good health.

I do love what having an exercise program does for me, though. It has lowered my blood cholesterol. It makes me stronger and helps me sleep better. I believe that I have firmer muscles in my thighs in my forties than at any other time in my life. I commit to exercise because I know it is a part of treating my body well.

I recommend that you start out with an exercise commitment that is not too strenuous. You could choose to walk around the block three times a week, then build up to walking three times a week for 30 minutes. Eventually, build up to walking fast enough to keep your heart beating at your target heart rate for aerobic fitness for 30 minutes.

After you've established an exercise habit, you should ask your doctor to recommend some weight-bearing exercises to reduce the risk of osteoporosis and other ailments. Osteoporosis prevention is a combination of adequate calcium and vitamin D intake, weight-bearing exercise, avoiding smoking and excessive alcohol, and monitoring bone health. Every woman should discuss risk factors and strategies for prevention with her doctor.

Make Over Your Shopping Habits

I've already mentioned making over your clothes habit. Much of overindulgence in clothes and food starts while shopping. In fact, you may find as you get your eating and clothing under control you have more money to use for eternal purposes.

Establishing a budget for your total household expenses is mandatory for managing God's money well. Even if you can't get your husband to support you in your effort to make a household budget, you can make a budget for the spending you do. Decide what is the right amount of money to spend on clothing and food, including eating out.

Next, you can make over your shopping habit by making lists. Most of us do this when we shop for food, but it is also very helpful when shopping for clothes. Before you go shopping, look over the clothes you have. Decide what you need and think about what you are looking for. When you shop, don't be distracted by everything you see, but have specific clothing needs in mind. It's okay to splurge occasionally, but it shouldn't be a regular occurrence.

When shopping for food, do the same. Except for the occasional splurge, don't buy items that aren't on your shopping list or don't contribute to good health.

I hope you learned some ways to care for your body from the other women in your group. Taking care of your body to glorify God brings true freedom and balance.

How to Help Others Develop a Healthy Body Image

Do you know a woman or girl who never makes a negative comment about her body? Probably not. The problem of negative body image is epidemic in American culture and the developed world. Christian women who have a healthy body image can be a beacon to others in the way they talk about, treat, and honor their bodies.

I've had opportunities to talk to secular audiences on this subject. Afterward, I am almost always approached by someone who asks if I'm a Christian. That person can see that there is something deeper than just human reason and knowledge that gives me the foundation for the information I share.

You may not teach or speak on this subject, but there are opportunities for you to get involved in making the world a safer place for girls and women. If you are a mother, your realm of influence is great. You need to be thoughtful, not only about the example you set for a healthy body image, but also regarding the words you say about your children's bodies. You can contact advertisers and boycott products that are specifically degrading to women. You also have an influence on the women in your social circles. Let's look at ways you can be challenged to be an agent of change in your world.

Like Mother, Like Daughter

Mothers have a unique connection to their daughters. Mothers need to be intentional about the way they talk to their children (both sons and daughters) about their bodies. From the moment a baby comes home, mainly mothers are responsible for caring for their bodies. They feed them, clothe them, and decide when a rash is a bug bite, hives, or eczema and determine the proper treatment. Children come to moms with aches and pains, skinned knees, and sore throats. Moms show their children how to bathe and brush their teeth. Moms fix hair and pick out children's clothes.

*I can't stand the way I have a little pouch
around my belly, just like my mom.*

Sometimes moms get so used to this role, they fail to let their children grow up. Moms also have a tendency to think that they are so much a part of their children that it is okay to talk about their acne, fat, and so on in a way that they would never talk to a best friend.

*What Do Kids Need to Hear from Their Mothers
About Their Bodies?*

There are several messages that you want to get across to your children.

1. You want them to know that they are fearfully and wonderfully made (Psalm 139:14). You know the saying, "She has a face only a mother could love." Well, all children need to be sure that their parents approve of their bodies. This is hard to do if you think your child is not taking care of his or her body.

Please don't underestimate the power your words have on the self-esteem of your child. I see a common thread in the women I have treated with eating disorders. Many had parents who put them on diets and tried whatever means available to make them look perfect on the outside. This backfires in your relationship with your child and usually becomes a block to your child's success and happiness in life.

Instead of being part of the problem, I challenge you to use your influence to impact your children positively. From the time they can talk, you can teach them that they are wonderfully made. You can talk to your little ones about their scrapes and bruises. Point out how wonderful our bodies are as you watch new skin develop. Get a book about bodies to read with younger children. Talk about your own body in positive ways. Children listen to everything you say. When you talk about how you look like a beached whale in your bathing suit, it has an effect on your child.

You want to be sure that you get across to your children that appearance is important, but not essential. It is not mandatory for your child to look a certain way in order to believe that his or her body is fearfully and wonderfully made. Teach your children to respect their bodies by the way they rest, exercise, and eat.

2. As your children grow, teach them that God knows their body flaws. You can teach your children to trust God with hurts, including pain about physical appearance. Encourage them to ask God what good could come out of their limitations.

"O house of Israel, can I not do with you as this potter does?" declares the LORD. "Like clay in the hand of the potter, so are you in my hand, O house of Israel." (Jeremiah 18:6)

It will be difficult to teach your children how to accept their body flaws if you haven't been able to accept your own. That is why it is so beneficial for you to do this study. Do you need to believe that God knows your body flaws and desires to be close to you and comfort you about any pain these flaws have caused?

I see parents harm their children when they try to give them everything. Children learn from disappointment. The worst thing you can do is to try to fix all your children's body flaws in order to help them attain beauty by the world's standards. Rather, teach your children how to keep their body flaws in perspective.

3. You also need to teach your children that their bodies are the temple of God. If your children are Christians, the Holy Spirit chooses to dwell in their bodies, which makes them very special. This is the reason the apostle Paul said not to join with a prostitute (1 Corinthians 6:15–16). Not only should your children honor God with their bodies by following God's sexual standards, but also honor their bodies by not criticizing and rejecting their own flesh and how it is put together.

Wordless Messages from Mothers

Now that I've talked to you about what you should be saying to your children, there's more for you to think about. I want to encourage you to think about the example you are setting. Are you a good example of healthy body image to your children? Are you content with your age, or do you think you need to look like your daughter's sister? Is your lifestyle in balance? Do you talk negatively about your body around your children?

Your example will speak louder than your words. How you obsess about or neglect your body speaks volumes to them. Children need to see and hear their mothers model love and care for their own bodies. Your children will be aware if your main pursuit is beauty rather than character, and it will impact them negatively.

How Can I Help My Overweight Child?

Almost without exception, the compulsive overeaters I deal with replay messages in their heads from their moms. Do you remember Christine from chapter one? She's the one who is overweight but has a healthy body image now. As I mentioned earlier, Christine remembered shopping for clothes as the most humiliating side effect of being overweight as a child. Her mother didn't hesitate to make comments about Christine's body in public. She was usually frustrated because it was so hard to find half sizes, and the prices were higher when she did locate them. Instead of a fun and exciting adventure, shopping was a humiliating and agonizing affair.

"That doesn't fit either? Honestly, Christine, I don't know what we are going to do!" her mother would blurt out loud enough for the whole dressing room to hear. On one fruitless trip, her mom tried a new store. She walked in with Christine by her side and queried in a voice that everyone in the store could hear, "Do you carry half sizes?" The distracted saleslady asked her to repeat. "You know, half sizes to fit her." Christine's mom pointed to her and everyone in line turned to look. "No," the saleslady answered. And Christine's belief that she was a fat, worthless nobody was confirmed as they plunged on to the next store.

> *When I lost my leg in a farming accident, I didn't want to live. Now I like to play jokes with my leg, and I realize that I'm special and unique.*

Christine's mom had good reason to be concerned about her daughter. Overweight children have increased health problems. It's not wrong to want the best for your children and want them not to face the social stigmas of being overweight. However, I advise parents of overweight children not to put them on a diet (unless there is a specific medical reason), but instead to make changes within the whole family system.

In helping your overweight child, the foundation of all your thoughts, actions, and words toward your child must be love, respect, and acceptance. Your child needs to know that you love him or her no matter what! Your love and approval should not be based on your child's body size. If your child is overweight, she is most likely experiencing some rejection by peers and even herself. This is why she needs your love and support all the more.

You can take some important steps to help your child.

1. Don't single out your child. You need to change the whole family's diet, but don't announce that it is because of your overweight child. Robin and Don adopted two children from Russia. The girls were only six months apart in age. Robin and Don had a very active lifestyle and they ate out almost every night. The restaurant food was fine for one of their daughters and did not cause her to gain weight, but it was different for the older one.

Robin and Don had to make some major changes if they were going to help their daughter have a healthy body. Both hated to cook, so they alternated weeks to cook at home. They got a diet from the American Heart Association and started to feed the family more healthfully. It was a difficult decision, but they were very successful in not saying that the changes were all because of one daughter. In the end, the changes benefited the health of the entire family.

2. Be active as a family. Another change Robin and Don made was to plan family fun that included physical activity. They took walks and rode bikes after dinner. The children were exercising, and they didn't even know it. Robin and Don signed the children up for dance lessons, and fostered their enjoyment of soccer and swimming. The older daughter decided to quit dance after two years, and Robin and Don allowed this. They didn't want to force her to do an activity that she didn't enjoy, but they also made sure she was not watching television and playing video games all the time.

3. Teach your family healthy eating habits. We have so much to teach our children as they are growing. We teach them important spiritual truths about salvation. We teach them to make their beds and brush their teeth. We teach them not to lie or steal. We also need to teach them how to eat properly. If we leave it up to their natural cravings alone, they won't have healthy bodies.

Our dog, Aggie, is a great example. He gets a balanced and very expensive dog food that will supply him with the energy he needs to meet his every physical challenge. We put his dog food out for him every morning, but he waits to see if any crumb will fall from the breakfast table before he will touch his dog food. He finally eats it as a last resort when there's no hope of getting anything else. He doesn't understand how bad our food is for his digestive system. He just knows it tastes good and he wants it.

Our children aren't much different. It's important to serve well-balanced meals and explain why we have chosen the foods we serve. We need to teach them how large a serving to take, how many pieces of pizza to eat, and so on. My mom was a home economics major. Every meal that she put on the table contained the major food groups. I learned how to plan for and eat a well-balanced diet by example more than by words.

You can involve your children in planning, shopping for, and preparing meals. Eat together as a family as often as you can. There is nothing I enjoy more than sitting down with my husband and two children at the dinner table. It's a time for connecting and talking about the events of the day in a less hectic setting. If having dinner together is impossible due to work, school, sports, or lesson schedules, perhaps you can make breakfast your family meal of the day. It may take sacrifice, effort, and planning, but you can make it happen if it is important to you.

It's hard to face the fact that I just
don't look the way I used to look.

Don't ever become the food gestapo by forbidding sweets and treats, but teach your children to enjoy these occasionally (Proverbs 25:16). Have healthy options available, and allow them to choose what to eat. It's wise to limit snacks to certain times of the day or a certain number each day. Teach your children to eat slowly. People who inhale their food don't have a chance to tune in to their bodies' signals to know whether they are getting full or not.

Let Your Voice Be Known

There is a great need for women to join together and let advertisers know how their influence is hurting women. As we have seen through this study, an unhealthy body image develops from a combination of many factors. One such factor is definitely the effect of media and advertising.

Dr. Margo Maine, in her book *Body Wars: An Activist's Guide*, encourages women and men to take a stand against the dehumanization of women's bodies in the culture we live in. She writes: "We must transform our society into one where women and their bodies will be respected and nurtured instead of abused and neglected. We have been talking about the problem long enough; we must move into action." Her book provides "ideas, action plans, strategies, and tactics to do just that."[1]

Her book is a great resource for anyone who desires to become an activist for respect for women's bodies in the media. But even if you do not choose to let your voice be known in the media, you do have a voice in the world of influence that you live in.

Be the Voice of Reason

In the introduction I said that I felt called by God to write this book. I am so disheartened by the vile and ugly things women say and think about their bodies. I've spent the time researching and writing this book to help women stop the downward spiral of self-hate. I can see what a waste of time it is to be plagued by that deep crease that formed right above your lip. There is so much more to this life that you will miss out on.

I hope you are feeling the same way by now. I hope you are fed up with your own body torment and that you long to see other women and girls break free from this destructive and ugly habit. Let's come back to a passage we looked at in the introduction, Isaiah 61.

The Spirit of the Sovereign LORD is on me, because the LORD has anointed me to preach good news to the poor. He has sent me to bind up the brokenhearted, to proclaim freedom for the captives and release from darkness for the prisoners, to proclaim the year of the LORD'S favor and the day of vengeance of our God, to comfort all who mourn, and provide for those who grieve in Zion—to bestow on them a crown of beauty instead of ashes, the oil of gladness instead of mourning, and a garment of praise instead of a spirit of despair. They will be called oaks of righteousness, a planting of the LORD for the display of his splendor. (Isaiah 61:1–3)

The Isaiah passage you just read describes what God wants to show us about our bodies. I know that Isaiah was speaking directly to the nation of Israel, which lived in captivity to the Babylonians at the time. The temple and city of Jerusalem lay in ruins. God anointed His prophet Isaiah to proclaim His love and care for the Israelites in spite of their circumstances.

These words also describe the spiritual freedom God wants to bring to us. When we are body haters, we exist without the sense of God's favor. Can you look in the mirror right now and proclaim, "I have God's favor in the body I live in, without losing five pounds or straightening my teeth"? If not, then you are not living in God's favor.

God wants to heal the damage your body hate has done to your life. He alone can provide the confidence and strength that are necessary to battle the comments and pressures that are all around you. God wants to comfort you and bandage your broken heart, release you from the captivity of rejecting your body, and proclaim His favor over you.

You will know that you have received this from God when you find yourself wearing a crown of beauty. Do you see yourself as God's daughter—His princess? Do you recognize that your beauty is in wearing the image of God, not in having a buff body?

God wants to anoint you with the oil of gladness. Is your life full of gladness, or mourning? There is a time for weeping. Jesus Himself wept (John 11:35). But are you mourning about legitimate issues, or are you mourning over your wrinkles, layers of fat, and ugly clothes? When you are living in the reality of God's favor, your heart will be glad. You will be glad when you become conscious of your body. You will be glad when you observe women with better figures. Your gladness radiates the unique and special creation that you are.

My mom always complained about how flyaway
and straight my hair was. I still hate my hair
and feel like I can't do anything with it.

Your countenance will become a spirit of praise. It will be like a garment that you wear. For too long, your face has revealed the despair you feel about how you look. Receiving God's favor will change all that. You will become radiant in the praise you feel for your God and the way He made you.

You will become a voice of reason in the circles in which you associate. You may not be called to write a Bible study about body image or speak publicly on this subject. But you will have opportunities to speak to your children, your neighbors, your coworkers, and your circle of friends. You can be a voice of reason when you see women succumbing to disparaging remarks about their bodies. You can encourage, pray for, and love other women, as God has loved you.

Your Work and God's Work

One of the most difficult spiritual journeys for me is to let God do His part, while I focus on my part. Whatever God commands in His Word, He never asks us to do on our own. He simply asks us to be willing to let Him work through us. This is true in forgiveness, loving others, prayer, and even receiving a healthy body image.

Daniel is a great example of how to let God be God. In the following verses from Daniel 1, underline what Daniel did (the verbs that describe his actions). Circle the things that God did.

But Daniel resolved not to defile himself with the royal food and wine, and he asked the chief official for permission not to defile himself this way. (1:8)

Now God had caused the official to show favor and sympathy to Daniel. (1:9)

To these four young men [Daniel, Shadrach, Meshach, and Abednego] God gave knowledge and understanding of all kinds of literature and learning. And Daniel could understand visions and dreams of all kinds. (1:17)

And Daniel remained there until the first year of King Cyrus. (1:21)

In these scriptures Daniel resolved to follow God, ask the official for permission to eat certain foods, and remain where God had placed him. God caused the official to show favor to Daniel, and it was God who granted the knowledge and ability to understand visions.

Like Daniel, our part is to resolve in our hearts to follow God, take actions consistent with that decision, and remain where God has placed us. He is the one who gives us favor with others and gives us the wisdom, knowledge, and gifts that we need to fulfill the tasks He gives us.

Here is one closing thought about our bodies from God's Word:

Now we know that if the earthly tent we live in is destroyed, we have a building from God, an eternal house in heaven, not built by human hands. Meanwhile we groan, longing to be clothed with our heavenly dwelling, because when we are clothed, we will not be found naked. For while we are in this tent, we groan and are burdened, because we do not wish to be unclothed but to be clothed with our heavenly dwelling, so that what is mortal may be swallowed up by life. Now it is God who has made us for this very purpose and has given us the Spirit as a deposit, guaranteeing what is to come.

Therefore we are always confident and know that as long as we are at home in the body we are away from the Lord. We live by faith, not by sight. We are confident, I say, and would prefer to be away from the body and at home with the Lord. So we make it our goal to please him, whether we are at home in the body or away from it. For we must all appear before the judgment seat of Christ, that each one may receive what is due him for the things done while in the body, whether good or bad. (2 Corinthians 5:1–10)

My prayer for you is that you will grow closer to God year by year. In that intimacy with God, I pray that you will discover the rich beauty that He created in you. I pray that you will exhibit that beauty to the people in your world, and that they would want to know Him the way you do. I pray God's richest blessings over your life, and that you will give Him praise because you are indeed beautiful!

Help for Those with Deeper Issues

This study may have made you realize just how much a poor body image has affected your life. As you have probably noticed, it's rare to find anyone who doesn't think that something is unattractive about her body. This is a common problem. But some problems associated with poor body image need more help and attention than this book and a study group can provide. Of course, not everyone has developed addictions and destructive behaviors due to a poor body image, but don't feel discouraged if you have. Do get help for yourself and those you love. Though these are deeper problems, they are not unsolvable problems.

Eating Disorders

Compulsive Overeating

Women who find themselves addicted to food feel that they are moral failures. They have a sense that if they had more self-discipline this problem would instantly go away. They are ashamed to get help and many times don't feel that they deserve help.

Help is available. Maybe you feel that you've tried everything and there is just something different about you. That is not true. Jeremiah 29:11–14 promises that God has a plan for you and that you will find it when you search for Him with all your heart. God does want you to learn how to turn your addiction to food into dependence on Him.

Women have overcome their addiction to food in a variety of ways. It is not the tool (Weight Watchers, First Place, and so on), it is the relationship with God that makes the biggest difference. Don't give up! Seek guidance and counsel.

Confess your desire to overcome your addiction to a spiritually mature person who can give you support, and to a professional who can help you unlock the door to your food addiction. Doing this body image Bible study is a great foundation for overcoming the dependence you have on food. I hope you have come to accept your body a little more through the things you have written, what you have read, and the love and acceptance you have experienced from your group and God.

Do not seek out help with an eating plan to lose weight! Do it to take better care of your body. Eat healthfully out of gratefulness and appreciation for the gift of your body. Do it to take care of yourself, not to make yourself look better on the outside. It is good to have a bottom-line weight, a weight you won't go under, but don't have a goal weight that says "I am suitable to present to the world since I weigh this now!" In fact, it would be great if you threw out the scales and evaluated the results of your eating plan by how you feel (the energy you have) and how your clothes fit.

Anorexia and Bulimia

Like compulsive overeating, anorexia (compulsive restricting) and bulimia (compulsive eating along with purging the food with laxatives, throwing up, compulsive exercising, or a combination of these) are addictive behaviors. You need the help of someone, a professional or a group, to stop these life-threatening and destructive behaviors. There are many facets to this problem. A negative body image is just one aspect of the problem. Food and eating habits are not the problem; they are the symptoms of the problem. You need to learn how to understand

and accept yourself in order to stop the self-destructive behavior.

It's rare that those who have developed a compulsive habit of restricting food or controlling their food intake with exercise, vomiting, and so forth can break their compulsion on their own. Yet, part of the disease leads them to believe that it should be up to them. If you are one of those people, please ask for help. Reach out to a professional or self-help group.

An eating disorder is very complicated. This book will help you, but you need to come clean with a knowledgeable person who can lead you through the process and help you understand what has happened in your soul that causes you to focus all your energy on food and thinness. This person can help you discover that food and your body size are not the issue. Facing the real wounds of your soul is the issue, and you can't do that alone.

Helping Someone with an Eating Disorder

When you suspect your child or someone else you love has an eating disorder, you want to do something. God can use you to help that person get help. Often your natural instincts are to persuade him or her to eat more food. Some parents and loved ones even try to force the person to eat. This does little good. Here is a list of dos and don'ts that I share with people when they are facing an eating disorder.

Don't
- get into power struggles over food
- offer pat answers
- impose guilt
- blame yourself

Do
- lovingly confront the symptoms you see
- get support for yourself

- get professional help for family members under legal age; encourage adults to get help
- learn about eating disorders
- require the person to take responsibility for herself/himself
- talk openly and honestly about your feelings
- give honest feedback about appearance
- recognize that the problem isn't just food
- listen
- show love and affection

Body Dysmorphic Disorder

This is a real and growing problem. It is characterized by delusional obsessions with imagined or slight physical imperfections. It can drive women to depression, isolation from others, or suicide. Experts believe that it is under-diagnosed. There is help, and if you suspect that you or your child is overreacting to physical characteristics, you should seek professional help.

Considering Plastic Surgery

I do believe there are appropriate reasons to have plastic surgery. I am glad that there are so many skilled physicians whom God can use in the healing process. If you are considering having plastic surgery, think about it, talk to people you respect who can give you sound, healthy advice, and consider the options available to you. It is not a sin to have plastic surgery, but it is important for you to think through this decision and recognize what your goals really are.

Most procedures require anesthesia. You need to fully understand the risks and consider whether they are worth taking in your particular case. In the majority of situations, plastic surgery for purely cosmetic reasons is not worth the risk and money required.

Depression

Depression is characterized by a change in sleep patterns and appetite, overwhelming feelings of worthlessness, lack of concentration, lack of motivation, loss of energy, agitation, restlessness, irritability, and thoughts of death or suicide. Depression can be treated. It is important that you recognize the symptoms and seek help. There are many causes. It is possible to develop depression from constantly berating yourself and your body. If you have the symptoms listed above, please discuss them with your doctor or a Christian counselor.

Anxiety

Anxiety is characterized by intense worry, nervousness, panic attacks, and overwhelming fear of situations and circumstances. It can often lead to fear of leaving your home. As with depression, anxiety can be treated. You can overcome the panic and fear with the help of God, your doctor, and a Christian counselor.

Focus on the Family can refer you to a Christian counselor in your area. For a referral or to speak to one of Focus's counselors, call 1-800-A-FAMILY (1-800-232-6459) between 9 A.M. and 4:30 P.M. Mountain Time. If a counselor is not available to speak with you right away, please be patient. Someone will return your call.

Tips for Group Leaders

If you are leading this group, you probably already have experience leading women's groups, so I'll make only a few remarks specific to this particular topic.

Remember that body image is a painful issue for some women. Many have been deeply wounded by the comments of friends, family members, and even strangers. It is, therefore, extremely important that the women in your group feel a sense of safety and acceptance. No one should ever feel put down. As the leader, you will need to address any inappropriate comments so that spirits aren't wounded further. Make it a ground rule in the first meeting that no one will criticize another's appearance.

The questions in each chapter will be most beneficial if the women answer them in their journals. There isn't space in the book to write their answers, and the introduction suggests that they buy a notebook or journal in which they can keep their personal answers. We decided to publish the book this way so that readers would feel free to be totally honest. It also gives them a chance to share the book with a friend or relative without fearing that personal feelings or opinions are being exposed.

Participants will get the most out of the book if they take the time to read the scriptures (most of which are included right in the text) and write answers in their journals. They do not have to share anything from their journals in group time, but they may want to bring them to the meetings to make notes or to refer to if they do want to share from them.

Ground Rules

Go over the ground rules that are suggested in the introduction to the book. They have proven helpful in making women feel comfortable about what they share. Your group may want to add other guidelines.

In the first meeting, explain that this is the only time that women are required to speak and share information with the group. After this, it is voluntary. Some shy women might be intimidated by group sharing. In the first meeting, however, most should be able to give a little basic information about themselves. Begin by having them tell where they are from, how long they have lived in the area, a bit about their family, their work, and so on. Keep it light and short—nothing too personal.

Suggestions for Prayer

I encourage women to keep some kind of prayer list during group Bible studies like this one. A bond of intimacy develops as you pray for one another. Sometimes women use up too much time sharing details of prayer requests, and this leaves the group without enough time for study. One way you can avoid this is to have a sheet where each person can write her prayer requests before the session. If you have access to a copier during the session, you could make enough copies for everyone to take home to pray. Another idea is to use e-mail to share requests with one another.

Leading the Group

I have included discussion questions at the end of each chapter. You need to decide how you will use these in your group time. If you have a very talkative group, you may not be able to use all six questions.

Choose three or four that you think are most helpful from the study that week, then do the remainder if time permits.

You may want to write some of your own discussion questions. Some leaders will give a brief overview of the chapter before going into the discussion questions. Make sure that you spend time preparing your heart and listening to God tell you how He wants you to lead.

You don't have to teach this material. Everyone should have read the chapter, so if you do not feel gifted at teaching, don't try. If you have a gift for teaching and feel it would be helpful to the women, share your insights before discussion. I hope that you will see yourself as a facilitator. You are there to encourage discussion and learning. You can set the example by sharing first so others will follow, but don't do this every time.

Don't be afraid of silence. The biggest mistake leaders make is to be intimidated by silence. Silence doesn't mean that no one is getting anything out of the study. If you don't experience times of silence, certain women will never share. If you are particularly worried about silence, try counting slowly to 10 in your head before jumping in to share or moving on to the next question. Trust that God is at work in the silence.

Be sensitive to the women in your group. If you have someone who is shy, she will need extra encouragement from you as she shares. If you have someone who is taking over the group, be sensitive to the others. It is your job to make sure the group is helpful to everyone. You shouldn't be bashful about interrupting and redirecting the group if it is going in the wrong direction or if someone is dominating the discussion. Most of the questions don't have right or wrong answers, but if someone is sharing heresy or untruths about God's Word, you should gently but firmly confront her.

Notes

Introduction

1. Richard Foster, as quoted by James Bryan Smith and Lynda Graybeal, *A Spiritual Formation Workbook* (San Francisco: HarperCollins, 1993), 9.

Chapter 1

1. Located at www.plasticsurgery.org/news_room/press_releases/ 2005-procedural-stats.cfm.
2. ANRED Anorexia Nervosa and Related Eating Disorders, located at www.anred.com.
3. Kimberly Shearer Palmer, "Colleges Start to Realize Men Need Body-image Help, Too," *USA Today,* May 10, 2001, 15A.
4. "The Prevalence of Eating Disorders." Located at www.edap.rg/ edifo/stats.html.
5. Ibid.
6. "Coaching the Coaches," *Psychology Today* (March/April 1992), 10.
7. "Searching for the Perfect Body." Located at www.people.aol .com/people/ 000904/magstories/index.html, posted August 25, 2000.
8. Located at www.kidzworld.comsite/p. 3155.htm.
9. Ibid.
10. Ibid.
11. "Women spend two-and-a-half years on their hair." Located at www.dailymail.co.uk/pages/live/articles/news/news.html? in_article_id=402793&in_page_id=1770.
12. Located at http://www.christianity.co.nz/esteem4.htm.

Chapter 2

1. Margo Maine, *Body Wars: An Activist's Guide* (Carlsbad, Calif.: Gurze Books, 2000), 210.
2. Bruce Springsteen, "Better Days," *Bruce Springsteen's Greatest Hits.*

Chapter 3

1. *The Oprah Winfrey Show,* "New Medical Tests," March 12, 2001.

Chapter 4

1. "Researchers Discover Mind's Key to Self-Image." Located at www.aan.com/public/nrelease/05080, May 9, 2001.
2. Faye Angus, *Daily Guideposts,* 1993 (© by Daily Guideposts, 1992).

Chapter 5

1. Henry Gariepy, *Forty Days with the Savior* (Nashville, Tenn.: Thomas Nelson, 1995), 92–93.
2. Flora Slosson Wuellner, *Prayer, Stress and Our Inner Wounds* (Nashville, Tenn.: The Upper Room, 1995), 50.
3. Flora Slosson Wuellner, "Transformation," *The Weavings Reader: Living with God in the World,* ed. John Mogabgab (Nashville, Tenn.: The Upper Room, 1993), 31.

Chapter 6

1. Located at www.bodytalkmagazine.com/mixedlolies.htm, July 20, 2001.
2. Symeon the New Theologian (A.D. 949–1022), Hymn 15. Located at www.christianrecovery.com/library/body.html.

Appendix 1

1. Ron Blue, *Master Your Money* (Nashville, Tenn.: Thomas Nelson, 1991), 141.
2. For more information about the body mass index, go to www.nlm.nih.gov/medlineplus/ency/article/007196.htm.

Appendix 2

1. Margo Maine, *Body Wars,* x–xi.

How to Get in Touch with Dr. Deborah Newman

DEBORAH NEWMAN writes a weekly devotional on her Web site, www.teatimeforyoursoul.com. There you can subscribe to receive these free weekly devotionals, find out about her other books, book her for a speaking engagement, and get information about her speaking and seminar schedule. To contact Dr. Newman, write to drdnewman@ teatimeforyoursoul.com.

FOCUS ON THE FAMILY®

Welcome to the family!

Whether you purchased this book, borrowed it, or received it as a gift, we're glad you're reading it. It's just one of the many helpful, encouraging, and biblically based resources produced by Focus on the Family for people in all stages of life.

Focus began in 1977 with the vision of one man, Dr. James Dobson, a licensed psychologist and author of numerous best-selling books on marriage, parenting, and family. Alarmed by the societal, political, and economic pressures that were threatening the existence of the American family, Dr. Dobson founded Focus on the Family with one employee and a once-a-week radio broadcast aired on 36 stations.

Now an international organization reaching millions of people daily, Focus on the Family is dedicated to preserving values and strengthening and encouraging families through the life-changing message of Jesus Christ.

Focus on the Family Magazines

These faith-building, character-developing publications address the interests, issues, concerns, and challenges faced by every member of your family from preschool through the senior years.

| Focus on the Family **Citizen®** U.S. news issues | Focus on the Family **Clubhouse Jr.™** Ages 4 to 8 | Focus on the Family **Clubhouse™** Ages 8 to 12 | **Breakaway®** Teen guys | **Brio®** Teen girls 12 to 16 | **Brio & Beyond®** Teen girls 16 to 19 | **Plugged In®** Reviews movies, music, TV |

FOR MORE INFORMATION

 Online:
Log on to www.family.org
In Canada, log on to www.focusonthefamily.ca

Phone:
Call toll free: (800) A-FAMILY (232-6459)
In Canada, call toll free: (800) 661-9800

 BP06XFM